THE MURDER OF Minnie Callan

TOM GRUCHY

THE MURDER OF Minnie Callan

A TRUE NEWFOUNDLAND CRIME STORY

FLANKER PRESS LIMITED
ST. JOHN'S

Library and Archives Canada Cataloguing in Publication

Gruchy, Tom, 1948-, author
   The murder of Minnie Callan / Tom Gruchy.

Issued in print and electronic formats.
ISBN 978-1-77117-711-5 (softcover).--ISBN 978-1-77117-712-2 (EPUB).--
ISBN 978-1-77117-713-9 (Kindle).--ISBN 978-1-77117-714-6 (PDF)

   1. Callan, Minnie, 1925-1986. 2. Murder--Investigation--Newfoundland
and Labrador--Norman's Cove. 3. Murder--Newfoundland and Labrador--
Norman's Cove. I. Title.

HV6535.C33N67 2018   364.152'309718   C2018-904358-X
                                                   C2018-904359-8

PRINTED IN CANADA

MIX
Paper from
responsible sources
FSC® C016245

This paper has been certified to meet the environmental and social standards of the Forest Stewardship Council® (FSC®) and comes from responsibly managed forests, and verified recycled sources.

Cover Design by Graham Blair

FLANKER PRESS LTD.
PO BOX 2522, STATION C
ST. JOHN'S, NL
CANADA

TELEPHONE: (709) 739-4477   FAX: (709) 739-4420   TOLL-FREE: 1-866-739-4420
WWW.FLANKERPRESS.COM

9 8 7 6 5 4 3 2 1

Canada Council   Conseil des Arts
for the Arts   du Canada

Newfoundland
Labrador

We acknowledge the [financial] support of the Government of Canada. *Nous reconnaissons l'appui [financier] du gouvernement du Canada.* We acknowledge the support of the Canada Council for the Arts, which last year invested $153 million to bring the arts to Canadians throughout the country. *Nous remercions le Conseil des arts du Canada de son soutien. L'an dernier, le Conseil a investi 153 millions de dollars pour mettre de l'art dans la vie des Canadiennes et des Canadiens de tout le pays.* We acknowledge the financial support of the Government of Newfoundland and Labrador, Department of Tourism, Culture and Recreation for our publishing activities.

This book is dedicated to my loving son

SCOTT THOMAS GRUCHY
God's special angel
(September 8, 1967 – February 2, 1968)

and

In memory of

MINNIE CALLAN
Beloved wife, mother, and grandmother
(June 24, 1925 – March 13, 1986)

CONTENTS

PREFACE

Murder? Not possible. Not here in Newfoundland and Labrador. Murders just didn't happen in small communities where everyone knew everyone else. There were thefts, assaults, break and enters, and petty crimes that kept all nine RCMP members stationed at Whitbourne busy. There was always something to investigate, while keeping in mind that approximately ninety per cent of all reported crimes were committed by the same bunch—well-known local repeat offenders. Punks, as I liked to call them, high on either drugs or alcohol. They had no education, and for sure they were not university material.

In the 1980s, the very worst repeat offender was usually picked up in a couple of days, not like it is now. Our offenders weren't even smart enough to move out of the area. It was like someone placed a sign around their neck reading CATCH ME IF YOU CAN, MY NAME IS _____. You get the drift. They were definitely not the brightest stars in the sky. Like a yo-yo goes up and down, they went in and out of jail. I guess it must have been better than home. If one of them happens to be reading this, I apologize for being wrong about one thing—I'm actually surprised you can even read.

Like a cat-and-mouse game, we knew who they were. A handful of nobodies, too lazy to work and too stunned to do anything right. They didn't care about anything or anybody. We knew who they were, and they would always slip up one way or another, always get caught, and around and around the circle went. The likelihood of getting jail time was like winning the lottery—it was very remote, and they knew it.

These crimes weren't Elliott Ness–types of offences. They were considered more a pain in the ass than anything else, and the punishment reflected exactly that. In and out, another star, be a good boy. They all went to the tourist retreat in Salmonier, where it was compared to an all-expenses-paid vacation with friends, and yes, with relatives. Great meals, great accommodations, lots of leisure time. What more could anyone ask for?

Professionals? Far from it. They were the Newfoundland carry-on gang. This is absolutely no reflection on the majority of Newfoundlanders, who are far removed from the riff-raff. The Salmonier tourist chalet is closed now. But enough of that. Yes, we had plenty of petty crimes to deal with, but a savage murder, planned and premeditated by one of these locals? No way. I would have bet the bank on it.

Unfortunately, I would have lost.

THE VICTIM

Mrs. Minnie Callan
June 24, 1925–March 13, 1986

Minnie Callan was a stranger, and we probably would never have met in life. It's unfortunate that we did, considering how it was we came to cross paths.

She was born and raised in the area, Norman's Cove–Long Cove, grew up, fell in love, and raised a family—three girls and three boys—and loved them all equally. Minnie Callan was sixty when she died. She was young at heart and loved by all who had the pleasure to meet her. She was very well-known and respected: a wife, mother, and grandmother, living with the man she adored. They owned what they had. What more could anyone want? "Grow old along with me, the best is yet to be." That's the way it should be, but unfortunately that's not the way it always is. Fate has a say in the lives of everyone, and the Callans were no exception.

Much too early in life, Minnie's husband lost his battle with cancer. She tended on him hand and foot from day one, no questions asked. He passed away in 1984. The next few years would take the best out of her. He died much too young, and Mrs. Callan never really had the proper time to grieve before she also lost her life, in the most tragic way possible.

THE INTENDED VICTIM

A beautiful sixteen-year old young lady was spending the day with her best friend and not expecting anything untoward. Why would she? At sixteen, life is fantastic and full of excitement. How could she possibly know how close she came to March 13, 1986, being her last day on earth? And that someone else whom she most likely didn't know had taken her place? She never knew that the man who planned this was in the same house as she had been for the better part of the day. He had planned to rape and then probably kill her.

The young woman enjoyed life and the good things that it brought her way. Certainly the dangerous individual who was only a few feet away from her was the last thing on her mind. He had planned everything, from every minute she was with her friend, up until the time she left to walk home. Every step she took up that road was a step closer to her last. How could she know? Impossible. Guy Butt knew. He had everything worked out, or at least he thought he did.

Later, when the girl was told, she cried and laughed out of a mix of fear and happiness, as did her parents. They hugged and kissed. They knew they would never forget that moment. Fate, luck, divine intervention, or a combination of all three, had saved her life.

THE WITNESS

His life changed dramatically as he innocently walked home that freezing night in March 1986. I have prayed for him over the years. I am firmly convinced that he did the right thing, although he might not agree. There was no time to react—what he saw was forced upon him. He didn't ask to be there, but he was, and he did the right thing. Being young and scared, it was a natural reaction. He immediately called the police. There are some who would not have wanted to get involved and who would do nothing. I have met many like that over the years.

I admire him for his caring attitude and his honesty. He didn't hesitate to tell us exactly what he saw. The young man was instrumental in apprehending the suspect. I pray that he has looked at past events the way most have: that he was on the right side of history. He was also a victim here, and it is important we remember that. The eyewitness will always have my heartfelt appreciation.

THE VICTIM'S FAMILY

I know how the Callans felt. I've been there personally. We are all born to die, some with a lot more physical pain than others. I know this for sure, as I have suffered the loss of my first son, aged six months; my youngest brother, aged eleven years, in a car accident; my second brother, aged forty-two years, by suicide; and my father, aged fifty-six, died in his sleep.

I do understand, and I feel for them all. They will have to live the rest of their lives knowing that their loved one died in a horrible and unfair way. God bless them all.

THE PERPETRATOR

You have read about him here. I had to live with him for over three days and run errands for him. I never wanted to meet someone like him face to face, but it was forced upon me. I am reminded of a quote from the Bible whenever I think of the murderer: "Get thee behind me, Satan."

THE PERPETRATOR'S FAMILY

Mother, father, and sisters—there's not much I can say about them. Mrs. Butt, his mother, has made all her choices of her own free will and will have to live with the consequences. Let's pray that no one else gets killed. I genuinely feel sorry for her.

REVISIT OF SCENE

Life seems to go around in a circle. I felt that as I went back to the scene some twenty-five years later. It was my first visit since leaving Whitbourne. There were a lot of changes. However, I remembered everything as if it were yesterday. I had put off going back for all those years, but it was time. I took pictures of the area so you, the reader, would have a better idea. Nothing from the murder scene—from where he lived, to the slipway— has changed much. I walked the same route I did in 1986 and could see again what I saw back then. The difference this time was there were no surprises, no investigation, just me and my camera.

I stopped a lot, just remembering. My wife, Mary, was with me. As we walked the murder scene from the guardrail to the cliff's edge, I told Mary to be careful and watch her step, because I had fallen in this area on March 13, 1986. I couldn't see exactly where it was—the grass had completely covered the spot. No sooner than I spoke the words did I slip and fall backwards over the same drop! This time, high, thick grass broke my fall. The last time it had been snow.

Soon, we were on our way. That will most likely be my last visit to the area. I had finished what I set out to do. I pray that the family will find peace. I hope this is finally the end for me. I have had no dreams since I started writing. To the Callan family, I hope this helps you in some way. Have peace in knowing that God will not be mocked.

Sometimes terrible, unspeakable things happen to good people. Their story still has to be told.

Author's note: With the exception of Sgt. Art Slade and the author, Cst. Tom Gruchy, the names of the police officers herein have been changed to protect their identities.

THE MURDER OF Minnie Callan

CHAPTER 1
WHITBOURNE

A little about the Whitbourne Boys' Home. The home housed kids up to age sixteen, from all over the eastern part of the island, mostly from St. John's. The home was huge and almost always full. It was routine for RCMP officers to be called at all hours to search for escapees. Two or three times a week, in all kinds of weather, we expected it. It was a major pain, but it went with the territory. Just kids, no life before Whitbourne, and for the most part no life afterwards. The cost must have been staggering. I can only imagine. The government was on the hook for all the damages that were incurred while the boys were on the run and for which personal insurance didn't cover, likely a tidy sum. Most locals were prepared and on their guard when the boys were out, but there were never any confrontations between the boys and the locals, at least none that I can remember. They generally didn't go through town—too easy to be caught and brought back. A week in the hole wasn't something to look forward to, which was their usual punishment for walking away. Rather than "breaking out," walking away would be the best way to describe how easy it was: over the fence, down the rail track, right to Ocean Pond, where there was access to hundreds and hundreds of private cabins. Most times we had them back in a couple of hours. Sometimes it was much longer. Thanks to the police service dog, the latter was definitely the exception to the rule. The longer they were out, the more damage they caused. For the runners, it was not all wine and roses. The time of the year didn't make a difference. Generally they were all returned safe and sound with a slap on the wrist. However, one time the weather turned very bad, so bad that we had to call off our search—we couldn't see our hands in front of us. We hoped that this time they managed to get into someone's cabin, where they would be safe. Unfortunately, one didn't, and a young life was lost. He froze to death next to the tracks a few miles from the boys' home. It bothered everyone. Was there a lesson to be learned? For sure. But was it learned? No way. The running would continue. Some would make it home to St. John's, no minor feat in itself, just to be turned back in as quickly, either by a family member or friend. They were picked up and returned until the next time.

Most Newfoundlanders are familiar with Whitbourne, but probably not as familiar with the RCMP Whitbourne Detachment area. The boundaries start on the Trans-Canada Highway at Ocean Pond and include all of Ocean Pond and everything on both sides of the TCH to just past Bellevue, Whitbourne proper, Markland, Route 80 from the TCH down the shore, from Blaketown to Islington and every community in between, from Chapel Arm around the loop to the TCH, including Bellevue and all communities in between, and to Fairhaven on the southern side of the TCH.

There was, unfortunately, one other murder in Whitbourne proper many years earlier, which I am sure is still in the minds of most residents of Newfoundland and Labrador. Detailed articles have been written about this unnecessary tragedy. A young and very inexperienced RCMP officer, Robert Weston Amey, lost his life, killed with his own revolver while trying to arrest three escaped convicts from Her Majesty's Penitentiary in St. John's. Three who, after they escaped, found their way to Whitbourne. I often thought about it as I made regular patrols where it had occurred. What a waste of a human life, a very young man with all kinds of promise ahead of him, an RCMP officer, a first posting, a man with a family, not married but with a mother, father, sisters, and brothers, doing a job that he took a solemn oath to perform to the very best of his ability. Gone forever, and for what? Too many mistakes were made which cost him his life. That was well before my time. I knew all the details and the exact spot. I walked and drove by there many times, too many to count, and I always took a moment to reflect. Gone but definitely not forgotten. Very few, if any, ever talk about it anymore. They have their own reasons. There are no reminders, no pictures, no plaques—nothing. I guess we all have our own way of dealing with grief.

Everything considered, Whitbourne Detachment area was a great place to work, for the most part. The residents were friendly, easygoing, and easy to get along with. They respected the police and what they stood for, which was evident by the way they treated us. A great place to work, but of course there are exceptions to every rule. The exceptions know who they are. I am willing to bet that nothing has changed: once an asshole, always an asshole. Remember the old saying about a leopard and its spots?

But this is not about them. This is not about petty crime. It's not about Cst. Amey, the deceased RCMP officer, and it's not about the boys' home. It's about the most horrific, cruel, senseless, unbelievable, premeditated murder—a murder unrivalled even by today's standards. When you read further, you will understand and surely feel as I did then, and still do today, more than thirty years later. A murder, unheard of in the small, peaceful community of Norman's Cove, which was planned and committed by one of their own on that freezing winter's night, March 13, 1986, would be remembered by many for years to come. Some, of course, would never forget. A local murdered by a local.

Lightning did strike twice. Cst. Robert Amey, Whitbourne; and now Norman's Cove. Here in a community where life virtually comes to a standstill at midnight. All good people at home doing what families usually do with not many worries or cares. This night was to be much different. Lives were about to be changed forever. This night would be a reality check.

Word spread like wildfire from the very young to the very old. Some may have just brushed it off—they just didn't want to believe the unbelievable. That's just the way it is for some. Most, however, were scared to death. Rumours, just crazy rumors, some said, but not actually believing it, trying to convince themselves—*no way, not here* was the common remark. Understandably, no one wanted it to be true. This night in this very quiet, peaceful Newfoundland outport, entire families were destroyed.

CHAPTER 2
THE CALL

My shift started at two o'clock in the afternoon. I hoped it would be just a routine two-to-ten shift. That's what we all hope and pray for, a shift with no problems, just an ordinary, uneventful, routine eight-hour shift. It was exactly the way it started and ended, absolutely nothing out of the ordinary. On the way home, just more or less daydreaming, my thoughts went back to a year before, when I was on patrol then, as I was now, about fifteen to twenty kilometres down the Argentia access road. I passed a familiar location on the highway, one which was just as cold. I was heading home then, as I was now. I laughed at the familiarity of it all.

Not only was it very cold the year before, but it was also very windy. It was windy enough to blow a section of snow fence onto the highway. This was the type they place along windy sections of the highway to cut down on drifting snow. There it was, right in front of me, and it had to go. It posed a danger to other drivers who may not be lucky enough to see it. I was dressed for the night. As it was only about twenty feet from the front of the police car, I engaged the emergency lights, just in case, and threw the fence section off the road. I walked back to the police car, all lights on and the engine running. Well, it was so windy, the door slammed shut. I just wasn't fast enough. And just my luck, all the doors were locked. I panicked at first, and seeing no other alternative, I executed my last resort. A window had to go. The butt of a Smith & Wesson revolver can break a car window when struck hard enough.

When I parked the car for the night, it only had three windows. I would worry about the report later. For obvious reasons, I decided to keep the circumstances which caused the breakage a secret. But keeping a secret like that would prove to be impossible, so, over the years, many of my acquaintances had a great laugh at my expense. It could have been worse. What if someone had come along while I was locked out of the car?

Now I was home safe and sound. I was on call until 7:00 a.m. At Whitbourne we usually worked alone and were on call until an hour before the next eight-hour shift started. Little did I realize, in a couple of hours I would be facing a crime scene that would haunt me for the rest of my life. Hundreds of bad dreams. Nightmares. I never talked about that day to anyone. I couldn't. I just kept it all bottled up inside. Honestly, I was never as scared of anything in my whole life as I was when alone and doing my initial investigation at the crime scene. This time, I was scared to death.

I thought about another incident when I was driving back home, and again I laughed. Just a month earlier, I received a call from St. John's. It was an alert of an escaped inmate from Her Majesty's Penitentiary in St. John's: be on the lookout and approach with caution. I had a full description of the vehicle, and I saw it coming toward me, just after dark and on the same highway. Alone again, I called in to report I was stopping the suspect vehicle, which I did with gun drawn and with most of the road blocked. I ordered the occupant out with hands in the air. No problem—well, maybe just one. The only person more scared than I was the driver, the only person in the vehicle, who happened to be the magistrate on his way home from court. I promised myself over and over to never tell anyone. You're the first.

10:00 p.m. Home, a cup of tea, a drink, most likely the latter—and only one, as I was on call. The chill I had in my bones stayed with me for quite a while, but the drink helped. It was one of the coldest nights I could remember. Maybe it was the drink, but sleep came fast, which was unusual for me. Normally it took me a while to wind down. The bedsheets had a welcoming warm feeling about them. Getting in bed and curling up into the fetal position, skin against skin, cold against warmth, in no time I went into a deep and sound sleep.

Without warning, sounds, off in the distance, ringing sounds, ringing, ringing, and ringing, then quiet. Thank God. But the ringing persisted, over and over, and I managed to shake myself awake and have a look at the clock on my nightstand, which said 11:35 p.m. I turned to look out my window. Still dark. The phone kept ringing. I answered.

"Hello, Tom." I recognized the voice, but I was still not quite focused. "Tom, are you there?"

"Sorry, what? Yes, I'm here."

"Tom, St. John's Telecoms."

"Yes, yes, I'm here."

"Tom, we have you on call until 7:00 a.m."

"Yes, I know, I know."

"There was an anonymous call. You need to attend to this right away and get back to us as soon as you check it out. Tom, we think it's important, and very serious." The voice on the other end was noticeably anxious. "Tom, like I said, it sounds serious. Very serious."

"Okay, I'm on the way."

"Call us as soon as you check it out."

"10-4."

I sat on the edge of the bed for a moment and listened to the silence. I shivered for a second when I remembered how cold it was when I came home, and I definitely didn't want to go back outside. However, I had no choice, it was what I was getting paid to do, and in those days, $12,000 a year was really good pay. I don't know why I thought about that, but I did. However, this wasn't about money. What was important now was that someone may be in trouble, serious or not. So, on this freezing Newfoundland winter night in March, I was back on the road again.

In the previous fifteen-plus years I had responded to hundreds of anonymous calls, but this one would turn out to be much different. This call would bother me for a very long time and dramatically change the way I looked at things.

Being a born and bred Newfoundlander, an old Newfoundland saying came to mind. It was as cold that morning as a spinster's heart. As I stepped outside my house to answer the call, it felt much colder than when I had gone inside a couple of hours earlier. I wondered, was this just another anonymous call? Normally this could wait until the next shift, just six or seven hours away, depending on the nature of the call, of course.

Our telecom had nothing specific to go on, just the location and that a female was being assaulted. That was it. The caller, a young man, appeared to be extremely upset. Our civilian member on duty who received the call had a gut feeling, and that was good enough for me. They were rarely wrong. They were experts at what they did, and I had to respect that. However, I still hoped that there would be nothing much to it, like the hundreds of other anonymous calls. It was not unusual for people to overreact when excited, but this was not one of those times.

Walking to the marked police car parked in my driveway, I shivered uncontrollably and continued to do so for some time after, even for a while after the car warmed up, at which point I was well on my way. It was so cold that all the windows were as clear as they would have been on a summer's day. I was no longer sleepy. I was as alert as I had ever been. It's amazing the effect that ice-cold salt air will have on you. I was a mile or two from my house in Dildo before the car finally warmed up and the chill left my bones for the second time in as many hours.

God, it was cold. Living and working right next to the Atlantic Ocean didn't make it any warmer. As I drove up the shore from Dildo to the Trans-Canada Highway, I could hear the continuous crunch of the ice and frozen snow beneath the tires. All we used back then were either all-season or plain snow tires.

With road conditions the way they were, I knew it would take between thirty and forty minutes to reach the site in Norman's Cove.

CHAPTER 3
THE SCENE

With no police car lights activated, no sirens blaring, just the crackling sound of tires on the frozen snow, I gingerly left my driveway and headed up the shore. I turned right on the Trans-Canada Highway, to where I would come face to face with a shocking sight.

God, how peaceful it looked from inside the warm vehicle, to see the ocean on my right as I drove along. It seemed to swell up and down with the tide and the slob ice, which had formed because of the frigid temperature. My heart beat faster and faster the closer I got to my destination. Why in God's name, I asked myself as I drove along the deserted highway, would anyone want to be outside on a night like this? I felt kind of angry because I would have to go outside again. Especially since I had just finished a shift of eight hours.

Travel from my house to the reported area took me thirty-nine minutes. The highway was snow-packed, icy, and very slippery. There was no sand or salt; it was too cold for these to be of any use. On the drive from Whitbourne Junction, I felt the rear of the car slide from side to side. Several times I thought I would lose control and go off the road onto the shoulder, or worse. I was driving at what I felt was a safe speed, considering the terrible road conditions. The closer I got to my destination, the faster my heart seemed to beat. I prayed all the way—first, to get me there safe, and second, to let this be a prank call. I turned off the TCH just a few miles down this winding, slippery road, a road dotted with houses on my left and the open ocean on my right.

Thirty-nine minutes after leaving my driveway, a drive that would normally take less than twenty minutes, I arrived at the reported location of the attack. I stopped the car and, with flashlight in hand, looked around from all sides. Stepping from the car, the dry, frosty air really bothered me at first. Breathing was difficult, as it had been when I left home. The semi-frozen Atlantic didn't help one bit. The frost in the air seemed to bite into my exposed flesh. In short order, my moustache was frozen solid. It was like breathing crystals of pure ice. The moon was full and bright with a ghostly mist around its entire perimeter. The sky was full of tiny, brilliant specks that reminded me of one of those Christmas globes I had when I was a child that, when shaken, would fill the interior with millions of sparkles.

God, it was cold. I walked back to the car for a second to get my bearings. How I wanted to get back inside for just a minute to warm up a little, but I thought better of that idea. I thought back to my driveway, where I had still been just a couple of hundred feet from the Atlantic Ocean. At first glance I didn't notice anything out of the ordinary. I had an instant feeling of relief despite the freezing cold. As I searched, I was feeling more sure that this was just another crazy call, another false alarm.

Everything was quiet and subdued. I could hear the open ocean on my right, approximately sixty feet or so from where I was standing at the road's edge. A long guardrail secured the area, and I could see why it was necessary. I was to find out that there was a drop of about thirty or forty feet to the rocks and the icy ocean. I was familiar with the area, having driven this road many times while stationed at Whitbourne, though I'd never had occasion, the need, or the desire to walk from the road to the edge of the bank. Tonight, for the first time, I did.

As I stood by the car, I couldn't see or hear anything out of the ordinary. "Thank God," I said aloud. I couldn't leave yet, though, not until I was one hundred per cent sure that there was nothing to find. I was feeling more comfortable. To my left were two or three houses a few hundred feet away from where I stood, then nothing but trees. On the right was the sea, which extended all around that shore, right to Bellevue. There were no lights on in the houses and no sign of human activity. Several dim pole lights did little to illuminate the area.

Again with flashlight in hand, with the police car running and the headlights left on, I walked forty feet or so farther down the road, more or less talking to myself as I walked. I heard myself say, "That's good, nothing here," over and over again, as I turned to walk the short distance back to the warmth of my car and then home and back to bed. I remember looking at the sky and thinking how beautiful and peaceful it was. I stopped by the guardrail and listened for a second to the sound of the slob ice as it slapped against the rocks below. I remember thinking that God was great. I was also thankful and felt very lucky to be standing on solid ground.

It was then, during those few seconds of peaceful reverie, that my world as I knew it came tumbling down. It was then I knew that this had not been a nuisance call. I knew that someone had suffered terribly and probably died a short distance from where I was standing on the ocean side of the guardrail. Plowing had piled the snow against the guardrail to about waist high. As I peered over the snow, I was startled by the amount of blood spread over such a large area. It was proof beyond doubt that someone was seriously hurt, but where were they? Whoever it was, they were still there. There were no physical signs on the roadway, other than the ocean, and there wasn't a sound. I had to find them.

I prayed it wasn't too late. Suddenly, I didn't feel the cold anymore. My forehead felt sweaty beneath my Force-issued fur hat. Being alone was now less of a bother to me. I had a job to do, and I wanted to do it right. Everything that happened from here on in would depend on me. If this were fouled up in any way, I would have no one to blame but myself.

There is absolutely no beauty to be found in death. Why would another human being take another person's life? What satisfaction could there possibly be, and why should anybody have to deal with something as ghastly as this? As I wrote this, I stopped and asked myself the same questions I did then, and I still didn't have any of the answers.

I felt alone again, more alone than I had ever felt in my life. Suddenly, I was standing on the road side of this guardrail, and I was more afraid than I had ever been before. Even though I was a seasoned police officer, at that moment I had no idea what to do next. I just stood there for a moment, trying as hard as I could to focus. The car was idling just a few feet away. God, all that blood. I was trained to know how to react in the most difficult times, and there had been many, but this was entirely different. Damn. Why was this my night to be on call? Eight other members—what were the odds?

The roar of the ocean jolted me back to the moment. I had to do what had to be done. I was still not sure what I would find, but I knew in my heart it wouldn't be good. I climbed over the guardrail to the ocean side. I was careful not to disturb the crime scene. My police training and instincts took over. I had to do what I was trained to do: find the victim. I stopped again, turned, and wondered. Maybe I would find the victim a few feet away and they would be okay, hurt but still alive. I assumed from the start that it was a female I was going to find. A man never even came to my mind. *I will find her and she will be okay*, I told myself. And I did find her.

I walked slowly and carefully toward the ocean. I knew is was only a short distance away from the guardrail. I had my light, the moon was full, and the snow glistened and crackled as I walked, step by step, checking all sides as I walked to ensure I was outside the crime scene. I could actually hear my heart beating as I followed the blood. Then I saw a body imprint in the snow, indicating it was moving, or, more accurately, was being dragged, and I followed the prints of its outstretched hands. I could see the fingermarks—no gloves—just fingers and thumbs trying to grab hold to something, anything, as the victim appeared to be face down.

Deeper and deeper. She had to be close. *I know she is here, and I will find her.* I called as I walked, but there was no reply. There was one set of tracks walking outside the bloody body imprint, the toes pointing back in the direction of the road. I had to be close. Boots, big boots, leaving small blood droplets in the snow. She had to be here. I slowly walked in the direction of the ocean. The cold ocean spray was hitting the rocks below. I lost focus as I followed the imprint in the snow before I realized that the body impression in the snow was not as close to me as it had been. It seemed to be moving farther away to my left—it was still the same bloody impression in the snow, but it was moving away from me. Strange.

Then, suddenly, I was falling.

The flashlight flew from my hand and landed in the snow some fifteen feet to my right. The shaft of the light stuck in the snow, and the beam seemed to mark the way to the sky, as a trucker would put out a flare when in trouble on the highway. My hat fell from my head as my feet hit solid ground. It seemed like a lifetime had passed, but it was only a couple of seconds. I fell backwards as my knees buckled. I had no idea what had happened. All I knew was that I was a lot closer to the ocean than I wanted to be.

As I fell backwards, my back hit something solid and jagged. I spread my arms outward in a reflex motion, as if I were trying to take flight. I was afraid to move. Looking around in the darkness, I saw my flashlight. I had to get it. As I tried to stand, the back of my storm coat hooked onto something. I pushed away ever so slightly and could hear the rip of the garment, and my knee hurt from the six-foot fall. I was okay—I was safe. Slowly, I stood and walked toward my light. I had to have the flashlight. At this point it was more important to me than any other piece of police equipment available. I had to have it to see, to follow the body impressions, to where I hoped I would find someone, someone safe, and someone alive.

After retrieving the flashlight, I returned to where I had fallen. It was a sudden sharp drop, about six to seven feet. There was absolutely no way I could have seen it or prevented it. I had no idea it was there. Now I knew why the body impression was moving away from me. "Stupid," I said aloud. It had happened without warning. The person dragging the body obviously knew the area a lot better than I did. I was okay—shaken but okay. I was lucky the snow at the end of the drop had cushioned my fall. My hat was at the top of the drop, and as I put it back on, the snow from the hat fell down the back of my neck. The chill instantly brought me back to the moment, to the reality of why I was here. My heart was beating so fast I was sure it was going to explode. I took deep breaths to try to slow it down, but that didn't work. Even in the extreme cold, I could feel my forehead sweating. I wiped my eyes several times as one would if he was working hard in the midday sun. I walked, more cautiously this time, farther to my left, and less than fifteen feet away I saw the familiar drag marks in the snow. No change of direction, toward the ocean, not far now, only a short distance to the ocean wall.

"Hello," I called over and over as I followed the blood-stained impression. I removed my service revolver from its holster and held it in my right hand, the flashlight in the other. The hand marks in the snow were deeper. The trail of blood never changed. She had to be near, and so might he. I was ready; I knew what I had to do, what I had been trained to do. She, whoever she was, was my main concern. *She has to be okay; she has to. There's nowhere for her to go.*

Closer and closer I walked, as if in slow motion. My feet seemed to get heavier with every step. With my flashlight I continued to pan the immediate area in all directions. There was no one, just the body marks in the snow. No one, not a soul, just me, the impressions, and the ocean. I listened. Not a human sound. Absolutely nothing. The trail ended here. The area was open, and I could see that there was no one else.

"Hello," I called again, in vain. Nothing but the damn ocean.

I walked to the point where I knew by the sound of the ocean that I was not far from the edge. I looked to my right and there was nothing ahead of me but darkness. I stood motionless in the undisturbed snow on my side of the body impressions. There was no one. The snow was more disturbed, as if someone was moving around, but there was not as much blood. The ocean was close, so very close. Too close. I could smell the salt air. I had no perception where the snow ended—just a blanket of white and a dark sky.

Just a few feet more, and then I saw something different. Something I had never seen to this point: a set of tracks, large boot prints. At first I didn't realize what I was looking at. The snow was scuffed up, in an area about five feet around, near the edge of the embankment, then clear prints were heading back in the direction of the road. I didn't move for a moment. There was only one set, and they were too big to have been made by a woman.

"Jesus," I said aloud, but more out of frustration than anything else. I was angry, scared, and sick. There was nowhere else to go, nowhere else for me to look. I knew I would never forget the next few minutes for the rest of my life. It's been well over thirty years, and it still seems like yesterday. I had to edge closer. *God, please protect me, don't let me get hurt, please,* I prayed. I had to look and make sure.

Suddenly, the strangest feeling came over me. I was compelled to stop. Not another step. I slowly raised my light and looked outward. Nothing, just the sound of the ocean, the sky full of beauty, the moon bright, full, and clear. Nothing but the edge of the bank, just three or four feet ahead. I backed up slightly to get my bearings. There was that one set of large boot tracks again, walking from the scuffed area toward the road, just one set as before. There was only one place to look.

I inched forward, knowing the edge of the bank was only feet away. I decided I would stray no farther than the scuffed area. I had no choice but to look, and I did.

The beam on the flashlight was strong and clear. I immediately put my arm by my side, and the light shone on my rubber boots. Inch by inch I raised my hand, and my eyes followed the beam, slowly, outward and upward, not too fast. My heart felt like it was going to explode. Even in the cold, perspiration dropped from under my hat into my eyes. I still had my service revolver in my hand but didn't realize it at first. I placed it in my storm coat pocket and raised the light ever so slowly. I was no more than two feet from the edge, but still in what I considered my safety zone.

The beam of the flashlight shone straight out into the blackness. I prayed as I lowered it to the ocean floor, inch by inch, hoping against hope. Everything went through my mind in a flash: all the physical signs, the blood, body marks in the snow, one set of boot prints. As I lowered my light, there was more. It felt like I had no control over my arm. I didn't want to see. I wished and I prayed that this was a dream, but the cold always brought me back, back to the edge, back to the light, back to the truth. The beam from the flashlight was a little higher than the edge of the cliff, but my eyes were still focused straight ahead. I thought I saw a flicker from a light on the other side of the harbour, and I tried to focus on it. I was deathly afraid to look down.

I raised the flashlight, and my eyes were fixed on its beam. New batteries. How I wished for a minute that the beam was not so bright. I followed the beam, inch by inch, and suddenly I felt weak. My legs couldn't hold my weight. I fell backwards onto the soft snow. I fell, and I couldn't breathe.

"Jesus, God forgive me, help me."

I sat for a minute. My hand was locked tight on the flashlight. I rolled over and pushed myself up on my knees and got to my feet. I didn't move, not a step. I couldn't. Standing, I looked, and I saw a woman, the same age as my mother, slim. She had been beaten. Her hair was short, and the two-piece snowsuit she wore was purple and light grey. The bottoms were pulled down, and the top was around her shoulders—she was virtually naked to the world. She didn't feel the cold. She didn't feel anything. Her eyes were fixed on mine in a death stare. A stare that I would never forget. A stare that has stayed with me for over thirty years.

I wanted to be home. I didn't want to be a cop anymore. I didn't want to be here. This was not right, just not right. As hard as it was for me to look, it was just as hard for me to turn away. A very short while ago, her eyes had been filled with life and happiness as she went about her daily routine. Who was she? What was she like? Time would tell.

CHAPTER 4
THE INVESTIGATION

I sat in the police car and tried to take in everything I had seen. It was so warm I had to open the window and turn down the heat. I had been just a few feet away from where she lay. How much she must have suffered, but why? And by whom? It was just a little over an hour since I left home, and there was now so much more that had to be done. I couldn't believe this could happen to anyone. Was I scared? Not anymore. Hyper? You bet. I had to talk myself down.

I reached for the mic and pressed the dispatch button.

"97 [call letters for St. John's Telecoms] 97, car 215, 97-215."

A familiar voice answered. They were expecting to hear from me. Before I got out of the car, I had called to let them know I would be about twenty minutes. If I didn't call, they would send more police from Whitbourne to check on me. No need to say where I was or what I was investigating. They knew.

"Car 215, 97, go ahead."

"I need Support Services here as soon as possible. Tell the boys about the condition of the highway, and please call the Department of Highways and ask them to send out a sand truck."

"10-4," came the reply.

Telecoms knew what they had to do, but I told them anyway. "I need K-9 [dog section], Forensic Ident, and GIS." The latter were members who investigated major crime.

About five minutes later: "Car 215, 97, all requests completed and all units will be on the way as soon as they can get mobilized. They were advised to contact you when they get to Whitbourne."

RCMP policy dictated that all specialized sections must always have a member on call, as I was for the detachment. Further to that, I called back, "97, please call Sgt. Slade, NCO in charge of Whitbourne, and tell him the whole story and that I need every available member here as soon as possible. Tell him that I will need at least three vehicles and for them not to come in one car."

I sat back in the car and leaned my head against the headrest. For some reason I was suddenly very tired. Not just sleepy, but exhausted. I now realized it was going to be a long time before I got back home, so I prepared myself for a long night. The dome light was still on. I couldn't get her eyes, staring at me, out of my mind. I had at least an hour and a half before the St. John's crews arrived, and maybe forty minutes for Whitbourne. I had lots to do while waiting. I feverishly took notes about every little detail. Right now my first priority was to protect the scene. I was lucky because of the late hour, the area, and the weather.

The police radio startled me. "Whitbourne Detachment Cst. Gruchy."

"Go ahead Whitbourne."

"Tom, I just hung up from 97, and they filled me in on everything I need to know. I have five members and three cars getting ready, and they will be on the road shortly."

"Thanks, Sarge."

Everything was falling into place, just the way it should. Waiting would give me valuable time to finish my notes up to this point and to reflect.

My mind was working overtime. I was sure that a stranger had not been responsible for the woman's death. He was on foot and, because of the extreme cold, couldn't live far from the scene. I chastised myself for selfishly thinking about how inconvenient this was for me. What I had been through was absolutely nothing compared to what she had suffered. I would get home sometime, but this lady never would. Her future was gone. She lay dead just a few feet away from where I was sitting. She couldn't hear the water as it hit the rocks or smell the ocean anymore. The woman was probably in the wrong place at the wrong time.

Again my concentration was interrupted by the radio. "Cst. Gruchy."

"Whitbourne, go ahead."

"Tom, all members are on the way. They will park well behind your car, and you can walk to them with instructions."

"Thanks, Art."

"I will be in the office all night if you need anything."

"10-4."

The waiting was hard. I was anxious to get started hunting for the killer. My mind wandered back to the scene, as it would over and over again for the rest of the night. How could anyone be so cruel as to do this to a fellow human being?

I thought about the caller. Approximately 11:30 p.m. on a night like this. He had to live close by. The only way he could have seen the assault was to walk right next to the guardrail. Where had he come from, and where was he going? He walked by the guardrail, and he saw the attack. No one would have been able to see the assault unless he had been on the same side of the road. Maybe so close that he could see who the assailant was. It was a small community, and everyone knew everyone. Where could he be? He definitely held the key that would open many doors.

I stepped outside the car, leaving the window down and the radio on high. I walked to the middle of the road behind my car, to a distance of maybe a hundred feet. The icy sea breeze again bit my face. I shivered as I walked along, looking, not even knowing what I was looking for. Anything. But I found nothing. What did I expect, anyway? "Fuck it," I said under my breath. I turned around and walked back toward the car. I heard the crunch of every footstep I made as I walked on the snow-packed road. I walked along the road side of the guardrail. Still nothing. There was not even a latent boot print from earlier that evening, not that I expected any. I wondered, why would anyone walk home this way alone on a night like this? But then, at least three had: the victim, the murderer, and of course the witness, the main man.

Suddenly, I was shocked back to the moment. There it was,

right in front of me, just a couple of feet from the car and right next to the guardrail. I couldn't believe what I was looking at. It could belong to anybody, but very likely the witness. Not much to go on, but at least it was a start. It was a track, one single boot print, the right foot, and clear enough to be identified. A recent imprint. *Stupid*, I thought to myself. *I should have been more thorough.* I was virtually standing on it. Three people for sure had walked by here in the last hour or so. Two were immediately eliminated from the equation—the victim and the killer. I had the killer's print at the scene. It had to be the witness. A sound, a word, anything from him and this night might have turned out much differently. Maybe no one would have died.

I felt confident that it wouldn't be long before we knew who the witness and the killer were. I was still looking when the police radio broke the silence of the winter night, and I ran to answer.

"215, 97."

"Go ahead, Tom here."

"K-9, Ident, and GIS dispatched, ETA your point thirty minutes from now." There would be no radio contact with Support Services—there were too many privately owned police scanners. They were fully apprised by telecoms before leaving town.

"Please confirm arrival time."

"Will do."

I couldn't help but think about the victim and wished there were some way that I could cover her up. I continued to check around the area. I would be well-prepared when I met with Support Services. The scene would be secured. For a second I was happy that it was so cold, because there was not one snowflake—

ongoing snowfall would have been a severe impediment to gathering ground evidence. I walked several hundred feet down the road, on the same side of the road where the assault had taken place, and saw nothing. I checked for my own boot prints but saw nothing. Too cold, and the road had packed snow. I walked across the road and searched there, but still nothing. I thought about our service dog and was sure these were ideal conditions for him to track the killer.

I would talk to the occupants of the houses in the morning. There was no need to upset anyone at the moment. Things were quiet, and that's the way I wanted them to remain. There wasn't a light to be seen, and surprisingly, not a car had passed by since I arrived.

I stood on the opposite side of the road, just on the shoulder, forty or fifty feet from the front of the car, almost directly in front of the first house, which was set back maybe sixty or seventy feet from the road.

Then my heart skipped a beat. *No way*, I thought, *it can't be*. But there it was, right in front of me. I had no idea who the witness was, but now I knew where he went, and from where he had likely made the call. Another print, as large as life, the same right boot by the guardrail, leading to the first house past the murder scene and across the road. He went there, he called from there, and they would know who he was. I was one hundred per cent sure that the person who called knew the victim and the killer.

I was more than a little excited. I didn't notice the cold anymore. We would not leave this shore without the killer in the back of my car. I just knew it. While standing there, I tried to put myself in the shoes of the lone witness, feel what he would feel when he found out the end result of what he had witnessed. I thanked God I would never have to deal with that.

For a second, I felt sorry for him. The witness was either in the wrong place at the wrong time, or the right place at the wrong time. Whatever the scenario, there was nothing he could have done to change what happened after he walked away. He couldn't blame himself—he did what he thought was right at the time.

CHAPTER 5
THE ARREST

"Cst. Gruchy, car 219," blared out over the radio, "go local." That is a setting on the police radio that can be switched on when two cars are in close proximity to each other, and it usually cannot be monitored by the public. After switching, I spoke with the lead car of the three and arranged to meet, as previously agreed, no lights or sirens. The victim needed justice, and I needed help.

"ETA five to ten minutes."

A few minutes later, and within only a couple of minutes of each other, all police units were at the scene. One marked police car was positioned on the Trans-Canada Highway at the Chapel Arm turnoff. The officer was to advise motorists that they could not proceed past a predetermined perimeter area in Norman's Cove. There was only one main road from the TCH around the shore to Bellevue, with seven or eight communities in between. An alternate route was out the TCH to the Bellevue intersection and back in the opposite direction. The other two marked cars were stationed approximately a quarter-mile away, on either side of the scene. There were no side roads in between the closed-off area and only about a dozen houses inside, and we would deal with them in the morning. It was Saturday morning, and there would not be much activity. We hoped we would have the area clear no later than noon. It was important not to inconvenience the general public any longer than need be.

The first support unit to arrive was the K-9 unit, and right after that, Ident with one member, and GIS with two. They also had an unmarked car. All members were thoroughly briefed, and the wheels were quickly put in motion. They were all senior officers and knew exactly what had to be done. They were all impressed with the details I had gathered. This crime was as bad as it could get, and there could be no stone left unturned or any mistakes made. I was confident that with the help provided by RCMP Support Services, the killer would soon be apprehended. Based on what we now had, everything was in our favour. This was not well-planned, but it was a premeditated murder.

Nobody complained about the cold. Just police work at its very best. This was not the first time I had experienced this with members of the Force, but it was the most important. Ninety per cent of RCMP members, Canada-wide, will never experience anything like this. Back then we didn't use police security tapes, and DNA evidence-gathering was in its infancy. Crimes were solved by simple, honest-to-goodness police work.

I walked with the Ident member, pointing out things of interest. The first member was to catalogue the scene, so as to be able to give the forensics people an accurate picture of what happened. Time was of the utmost importance in solving a crime, particularly the first forty-eight hours. Sgt. Derek Bishop, NCO in charge of Ident, was the member on call. He decided not to go over and check the murder scene until daybreak, to ensure that he didn't miss anything on his first examination. In the meantime, he had a lot to keep him busy: measurements, photographs, and whatever else he could find.

The dog master, Cpl. Scott Damien, whispered, "Okay, Tom, let's go find a killer."

I said, "Great. I'm ready when you are."

The dog was straining on his leash, pointing straight toward the ocean. We didn't say a word as we let the dog lead the way. I was the last in line, the way it should be. Our dogs were unbelievable. I had seen them in action many times, with different handlers, and I was always impressed.

There were no houses on the left. There was a slipway with a small boat on it, and thousands of miles of Atlantic Ocean beyond. Tracks went around the slipway, and it was obvious to both of us that someone had tried to move the boat. The snow was at least eighteen inches high around the slipway, and it was flattened. Someone had tried to get the boat off and into the water but couldn't, as it was frozen solid onto its cradle. *Now what*, I said to myself. Scott led the dog back to the road, to the end of the pavement. Same routine, back and forth, back and forth.

In no time he had the scent again, the same scent, but back to where we had just come from, only about seventy or eighty feet from the edge of the road, to the very last house now on our right side, again straining against the leash. A two-storey house, back from the pavement forty or fifty feet, up a very steep, ice-packed driveway. We slipped as we walked toward the back door. The dog kept pulling on the leash. This was the best I had ever seen in a police service dog.

There was a front door about ten feet from the ground with no steps. I quietly said as we walked, "Watch out. That first step is a beaut." We both let out a slight chuckle as we went on. At the back door there was a porch built onto the side of the house. One step to the door, no different than any other step, except this one had a boot print—the one we were following. On this boot print was a large red spot, the size of a nickel. A blood spot belonging to the victim. We had him. We shook hands, and without a sound we left as we had come, without anyone knowing we had ever been in the area.

Sgt. Bishop, Cpl. Damien, and I talked for a moment. It was getting late, and they wanted to examine the murder scene. Sgt. Bishop wanted me to be with him as much as I didn't want to be, but this time I had company, whom I trusted. We walked maybe five or six feet to the left of where I had been when I arrived on the scene a couple of hours before. We walked on a forty-five-degree angle or so from my earlier trail, and I could still see every step I took. When I came near to where I had fallen, I could still see where my flashlight landed in the snow, as well as the prints I had made in the snow to get it back. That eerie feeling of what lay ahead came back to me, but this time it would not be a surprise. I had prepared myself, and I was ready.

We talked a little as we walked, side by side. I had hold of Sgt. Bishop's left elbow. We still needed flashlights, as it was what Newfoundlanders would call duckish. I guided him to where it was safe to stand. With the daylight, there was a much better perspective with relation to the edge of the cliff and the wide-open ocean. We stopped for a second and looked around.

"Just ahead now, to your right. Be careful. Can you see the edge?"

"Yeah, I got it."

Sgt. Bishop carefully examined each half-step he took. He stepped, stopped, pushed his foot solid into the snow, and pressed down on it. Experience is always the very best teacher, and he had a lot of experience, well over twenty years. Our main objective at any crime scene is to find and secure evidence. Ident's job was to examine it, photograph what they found, and bag it. They were forensics crime specialists. I knew what had to be done roadside, and I wanted to get on it. The warrant shouldn't take long. By the time the member got to Whitbourne, it would be ready. The highway had been saturated with salt and sand several hours earlier, which made driving a lot quicker and safer.

As we approached the edge, I couldn't help but notice that in this light there was a lot more blood than I had thought. I could easily visualize those dark, black eyes looking up at me, just staring into empty space. Again I felt my heart pound in my chest and the sweat on my forehead inside my fur hat. I didn't want to be here, but I had no choice.

Sgt. Bishop, in charge of Ident for the Avalon region, was like a rock. Cool, calm, and collected. I was impressed. He showed no visible sign of emotion. He had already seen and in-vestigated much in his long service, but I knew that it would bother him one way or another. I pointed out where I fell, and we both chuckled. As we pressed on, he continued taking pictures—no digital cameras back then, just rolls of film. I had my mind made up that I wasn't going to look at the body anymore. It wasn't necessary, anyway.

As he reached the edge, I stood to his left, and he slowly and methodically looked over. He saw exactly what I had seen. We both knew that the less we moved around, the better the evidence that could be gathered.

"Jesus," I heard him say aloud, and I wasn't surprised by his reaction. I didn't say anything. He stood and looked for the longest time, then looked back at me, and swore again.

Without any further comment, he went back to work and took dozens of pictures of the victim. His shoulder bag must have been full of small vials of film, and he went to it numerous times, changed the film, and wrote a description on the case. Soon, we returned from whence we had just come, covering our own tracks back to the road.

Sgt. Bishop had a lot more work to do before it was over. Full daybreak was only around the corner and would be the best time for his part of the investigation. In the meantime, the crime scene was secured, and nobody else would be permitted over the rail until Ident said it was okay. He had full jurisdiction of the scene.

We gathered together, and still no one commented on the cold. No one even suggested we sit in a car for warmth.

The five of us planned out our next move, one step at a time. We were lucky there was only one road through the community and that the Atlantic Ocean was on the right. Scott, the dog master, more or less let the dog go to the end of his leash, twenty-five feet or so. The dog sniffed up and down both sides of the road. It was obvious to the handler that the animal was reacting to my scent, so he directed him to the first boot print I had found, by the guardrail. Without hesitation, the dog left the first print and went down past the murder scene, across the road to the second print, then headed right to the front steps of the house. From there it went back across the road to the guardrail, to the exact spot of the assault.

Scott confirmed my suspicions that the person who owned the first print also owned the second and had gone into the house. He was still in there, or the dog would have continued tracking his scent. Was he the witness? The dog then left the guardrail, straining hard on the leash, to approximately forty or fifty feet down the road, and he stopped on the shoulder, roaming in a circle. We hurried over.

"Here, have a look," Scott said.

I stared in amazement. There, on the shoulder, was a small spot of blood. I would never have seen it. Scott called the GIS members and pointed it out to them, who in turn told Sgt. Bishop.

Cpl. Scott Damien said, loud and clear, "If he didn't get in or on any type of vehicle, Max will find him, I guarantee it." Cpl. Damien was good, and so was his dog. "Come on, Tom, let's go find him."

I followed, walking behind and off to the side, the way I was taught. The dog didn't need any new fresh scent.

"Scott, he's here. I know it."

"Yeah, Max will find him. Watch."

Taking note of the way the dog was reacting, we both knew we were close. The man lived here, somewhere close by. The marked police car was just where it was supposed to be. We hurried passed it, and the dog led us down a side road. Scott had to hold him back, yet he encouraged him as he went. A couple of hundred feet farther, we found another small droplet of blood. Just a small speck of blood. We lifted a safety cone we had borrowed from the car and placed it over the blood spot. There were about fifteen houses on this side of the road, and absolutely no activity.

"Tom, everything is going good for us so far."

We passed the last houses.

"Where is this going?" Scott asked.

"Right to the ocean," I replied.

"Great," he grumbled.

Max wanted to go, so we obliged, right down past the houses to the road's end. Nothing in front of us but water for hundreds and hundreds of miles. I couldn't believe it. Where was he? I didn't say a word. My mind was working overtime. Nothing there but a small slipway, hidden in the alders. The area around it was beaten down, and there was a small wooden boat lying on it. It was upside down and frozen solid. I tried to lift it and knew it was impossible. The snow around the slipway was well trampled. Kids might have done that, but Scott knew better, and so did Max.

"Tom, someone tried to get the boat off, and not that long ago."

He motioned the dog back to where the road ended, and immediately Max took off back up the street, maybe forty or fifty feet, before circling again. No blood. He went directly up a steep gravel driveway in front of the very last house on the left side of the road coming toward the water, now on our right. There were no lights on in the house. It was sixty or more feet from the edge of the road, with a steep walkway leading to a back porch door. The front door had no steps, and with the incline in front of the house, the door was at least ten feet off the ground. The dog went right to the back porch door. On the dirty snow, there it was, all the proof we needed—a spot of blood about the size of a nickel.

Scott whispered, "We got him."

He pulled sharply on the leash, the dog simply turned, and we all went back the way we had come.

"Come on," he said, "let's get the paperwork done and get the bastard."

On the way back, we stopped and gave each other half a dozen high-fives. The dog jumped, as if he knew why we were so happy. Scott gave him several treats. I realized then that, all this time, Max had never made a sound. We filled in the member on guard duty at the other end of the road and went up the hill, back to the scene. We could barely contain our excitement.

Five minutes later, we were back to where we started, back at the road. While we were searching with the dog, we couldn't use our portable radios. Our transmissions could be heard a long way off. The less commotion, the better.

Cpl. Damien outranked me, but this was my file. I did all the talking. I was excited but managed not to show it. I filled everyone in, and they listened to every word. After a lot of well-deserved handshakes, we went on to the next step, identifying the suspect. We knew exactly what we had, but it was no good without a name. No name, no warrant, simple as that. He had to be identified.

There were only two people who could give us the information we needed. Unfortunately, one was dead, but we felt confident we knew where the second one was, the anonymous caller, the witness. Who was the killer? We needed a name. I knew I could knock on any door and find out in a heartbeat who lived in that house at the end of the road, but that wouldn't put him at the scene. That would not be enough to get a warrant. We had to have the witness. We all felt he was the key. With his evidence, we could easily get the warrant we needed—that is, if indeed he saw what we thought he had, and if he could identify the assailant. My patrol area, my file, my move: the contact was left to me.

This time I stood at the bottom of the six steps leading to the front door with a different agenda. To say I was nervous would be an understatement. Me and the front door. I took a long, deep breath and raised my hand to knock. But I never hit the door; my fist hit nothing but air. Just as I was about to knock, the door opened. I got a bigger start than the young man standing in the doorway. By instinct, I dropped back a step.

"Hi," we both said at the same time. "Hello," we both said. Awkward.

He blurted, "I was waiting."

"Sorry," I said in return.

"I was waiting for you to knock on the door." That struck me as odd, but before I could respond, he asked, "How is she? Sorry. God," he went on. "I'm so sorry. I was scared to death. I wish I had my time back."

"Why?" I asked.

"God I'm sorry, so very sorry," he said again. The pain in the young man's face was easy to read.

"Sorry for what? You didn't do anything. Can I come in for a few minutes?"

I had to gain his confidence, and I was sincere—I felt for him, and I was glad I wasn't in his shoes.

"Can we talk? I'm Cst. Gruchy, RCMP, Whitbourne."

He stepped aside and walked to the chesterfield in the main room, and I followed. As we walked, I asked him his first name.

"Paul. Yeah, my name is Paul."

"Not sure if you heard mine, but it's Tom."

"Hi, Tom."

"Listen, Paul, I'm sure you know why I'm here. What you saw or didn't see is very important, as I'm sure you realize."

"Yeah, I think I do. How is she?" he asked again. "Who is she? I was afraid."

"Paul, listen. Never mind that now. Put it out of your head. You don't need to concern yourself with anything like that. Let me worry about it. You're okay, and you did the right thing. Paul, you have to trust me, okay?"

"Yeah, okay."

Still, when he looked at me I could see many unanswered questions in his eyes. I had to get by that or we would be in trouble.

"Paul, I have to know what you saw. One step at a time, Paul. This is very, very important."

"I called your office again, Constable. I hope she's okay. Is she?"

I didn't answer. He was way beyond scared. I tried my best to assure him and make him feel comfortable with me.

"Are you here alone?"

"No, Mom's asleep, and Dad is working away and will be home next Friday."

"How old are you, Paul?"

"Seventeen."

"Is your mom aware of what's going on?"

"No, she was asleep when I got in, and I let her know I was home, and then I called your office."

"Okay. Do you want to let her know what's happening?"

"I will, but not now. I'm okay."

"Well, as long as you're sure."

"Yeah, I'm sure."

We were seated directly across from each other in the dark sitting room. The only light came from the breaking dawn.

Head down, he said, "What could I have done? God, I'm so sorry."

"Paul, listen. This is not your fault."

"I was walking home, as I always do. Because of the turn in the road, I always walk that side and cross the street when it's safe."

"Paul, I know that right now you probably won't believe me, but everything is going to be okay. Trust me. There is something that I have to know, and I'm hoping that you can help me. Now, take your time. This is very, very important. Paul, do you know who they were? I have to know."

Silence at first. He looked up, and I could see that his eyes were glassy, as if he was about to cry. His voice quivered as he spoke.

"Constable, I never got a look at the lady. Her face was covered with either a hat or a hood. She was on her back in the snow, and she was crying or moaning. I can't remember. He was straddled across her waist."

As painful as it was for Paul, I needed to know what he knew in order to move on with the investigation. Time was of the utmost importance.

"Paul, please, I need to know."

I couldn't wait much longer. I stood up, walked over to him, and sat next to him on the sofa. Without hesitation, I laid my hand on his shoulder.

"Paul, did you know them?"

"No."

I was surprised. It wasn't what I wanted to hear. Everyone knew everyone in small communities like Norman's Cove, and I had been counting on him to identify the woman's assailant.

"I didn't know her, like I said. I couldn't see her. As I walked by, he looked at me, just for a second. He looked at me, and I knew him right away. I really don't think he even noticed me. He lives with his parents down the cove. I don't have to see him, do I?"

Excited now, but doing my best not to show it, I assured him that he wouldn't have to see the man.

"Paul, who was it?"

After a brief pause—one which seemed like an eternity—he mumbled something.

"Who was it?"

He looked at me, head high, and this time with confidence he said, "It was Guy Butt. It was Guy Butt."

"Paul, are you sure? You know how very important this is."

"I'm one hundred per cent positive it was him. Like I said, he lives with his parents, down the cove, they call it." He added, without prompting, "I believe he's married, or at least living with someone. I'm not sure if they are married or not. I don't know her first name, but I have seen her around a bit with him. He's a strange guy, and usually on the booze. I never did trust him. I think he would be capable of anything at any time. I just walked by. I was afraid. I didn't know what to do except call the police. Maybe I shouldn't have. I'm not sure what I should have done. It's too late now. I was going to call your office again, I really was.

"I saw most everything you were up to, and where you were there by yourself, I figured the lady was okay and had gone home. I saw him where he got back over the guardrail and walked down the road, I guess to his house. What will he do to me? Who was the women? What did he do to her? Is she okay?"

He would find out all the answers soon enough, but not right now. Before leaving, I shook his hand and told him that he should try to get a little sleep, and that we would be back later in the day to get a detailed statement. There was just too much to do right now and I couldn't hang around. We had what we needed. Getting a warrant would be no trouble.

"Whitbourne Detachment, car 215."

"Car 215, Whitbourne on local."

"We need a warrant."

"Right on," said the non-commissioned officer, Sgt. Slade, loud enough for the others standing outside the car to hear. "Good work. Give me the details." The wheels of justice were turning now, and gaining momentum as if going downhill. I knew that Sgt. Slade wouldn't waste any time. One of the GIS members left to pick up the warrant. A Justice of the Peace at Whitbourne heard the preliminary evidence from the member and was satisfied without any doubt that he was justified in issuing the warrant.

At 7:15 a.m. we were all together, back at the scene. The sentry police vehicle had done an excellent job redirecting traffic. Not a vehicle or a civilian entered the protected area. The area would be free to travel in five or six hours, as soon as the body was removed. The Whitbourne volunteer fire department had been advised by Sgt. Slade and were on standby.

Everything was in place and ready to go. We had a brief meeting back at the scene and were ready to execute the warrant. It was decided that three members were enough. I was one, along with GIS Cpl. Solomon ("Call me Sol or don't talk to me") Taylor and Cpl. Damien with our PSD, Max. The others remained at the scene and were just minutes away if needed.

Cpl. Sol Taylor and I stood on the doorstep. Cpl. Damien remained ten to fifteen feet off to the side with Max, who this time was on a very short leash. There was no doorbell, which was not unusual in an outport. Whoever answered the door would see by my uniform what I represented. I knocked several times and soon noticed a bright light through a side window. In short order, the door to the porch was opened. There stood a frail-looking older man, very short and very thin. He looked sleepy, and why wouldn't he? It was just after seven thirty in the morning on a Saturday, when most people looked forward to having a lie-in.

I introduced myself and asked him if he was Mr. Butt.

"Yes. What's the matter? What's going on?"

He looked directly at me, confused. I asked him if Guy was at home and told him we had a warrant for his arrest.

"What? Come in, come in, close the door behind you."

We did, after Cpl. Damien and Max came to the porch. As we stood in the large outport kitchen, I asked a second time if Guy was home.

"Yes. What did he do now?"

I repeated we had a warrant for his arrest and handed it to him to read. The older man walked toward a side bedroom, pointed to the door, and motioned to open it.

"That's fine. Thank you," I whispered, and we walked past him to the room. I glanced back for a second to see Mr. Butt trying with great difficulty to read the warrant. I could imagine how confused he must have been. A voice in a back room called his name several times, asking what was going on.

The bedroom door was closed. I slowly opened it and couldn't see a thing. It was as dark as a dungeon. With the help of my trusty flashlight, I immediately located the light switch, which was right where you would expect it to be, on the left side just inside the door. Cpl. Taylor had drawn his snub-nosed .38 service revolver. Mine was still in my Sam Browne belt. It was what we had decided—someone needed to have two hands free. Cpl. Damien waited in the porch with the dog, just in case.

Not a sound from inside the room. Without hesitation, I flipped the light switch on. The room was about ten feet wide and fourteen feet long, with a double bed, one small dresser on its side, and no nightstand or light. I didn't have time to think about the rest of the family, although I would see them all in short order. Not the way I would have hoped.

I saw two people in bed. A woman jumped from her sleep and screamed—thank God she was dressed, in one of those nightgowns women wear. It totally covered her body from neck to below her knee. She sat up in the bed. I will never forget the look on her face. I felt sorry for her, but it had to be done this way. She jumped out of bed, screaming, and ran toward the open bedroom door. No one tried to stop her—we weren't interested in her at the moment. She continued to scream for a long time, and I couldn't make out the words.

"Guy Butt, you are under arrest for the murder of persons unknown, and we have a warrant." That was the law. The accused had to be advised why he or she was being detained.

By this time, all occupants of the house were awake and in the kitchen. Cpl. Damien gently tried to calm them and did a great job keeping them away from the bedroom. One thing we didn't need was a hysterical family member in the way. We had to remain focused and leave the way we came in, but this time we would have one extra person—in cuffs. His missus ran, and we let her go for the time being. I couldn't see her, but we could certainly hear her.

Guy Butt was shouting. He stank of old, stale booze. Suddenly, he was running toward us, full throttle. This was not going to be easy. It was obvious he had no weapon, so Cpl. Taylor holstered his. Guy was also fully dressed, but not for bed like his companion—he was wearing a one-piece snowsuit.

"What the fuck are you doing in my bedroom?"

Guy had torn the bedclothes off the bed. The smell of booze

was nauseating. He ran at us, and we both jumped him at the same time. He fought and swore; we knocked over furniture as we wrestled him to the floor. In short order, he was face down. I grabbed his arms, one at a time, as Cpl. Taylor had his knee in the middle of his back. If he struggled any more, he would only hurt himself. We stood him up, and I read him the police caution.

"You need not say anything, you have nothing to fear from any threat whether or not you say anything, and anything you do say will be used as evidence. Guy, do you understand this caution?"

"Fuck off. What murder? You're fucking crazy. I was home all night. Ask the wife."

There were many questions from the family, one member after the other. They were treated politely and were advised that all their questions would be answered later in the day. Finally, they just held each other in the middle of this large eating area, watching and not saying anything else.

Our objective was to get him out of the house, in the police car, and back to Whitbourne. Snowsuit, socks, everything but boots. He walked the short distance from the house to the car in his stocking feet, and he calmed down when he saw the dog staring at him.

Guy sat in the back of my car. As was standard practice, I repeated the same police caution. He was more settled now, and this time he said he understood.

"I didn't do anything. You broke into my house. Tell you right now, you're going to pay for this."

During the rest of the drive to Whitbourne, not one word

was spoken. I couldn't help but wonder why he had gone to bed with his snowsuit on. I figured he was so drunk he probably passed out. The ride to my detachment was relatively short. The temperature was considerably warmer, with no clouds anywhere, and the road was wet and sloppy from heavy layers of salt and sand.

Like I said, the ride to the detachment didn't take very long, but to me it seemed like I was driving across the whole island. It would be a long time yet before I would pull the covers over my head. I was too excited to even care. I certainly didn't need anything to help keep me awake.

CHAPTER 6
THE INTERVIEW

On arrival, the detachment was lit up like a Christmas tree. I felt a sense of justifiable pride. Most all the other members were there, except the three sentries, and they would be there until Ident released the scene later in the day. All were maybe just a little envious, now probably wishing they had been on call. We had our suspect in custody, and in very short order, at that. A few short hours after the attack, we had him. He was secured in our only detachment cell with an officer on guard outside the locked door, with an understanding that there was to be no communication in any way, shape, or form, and to record verbatim anything he might say in relation to the charge. We would prove him guilty beyond any reasonable doubt. I was sure of it, but for the time being he was innocent until proven guilty. Anything could happen.

Sgt. Bishop, Cpl. Damien and one GIS member were still collecting evidence at the scene. The Whitbourne fire department would be called as soon as Ident was finished at the murder scene. Cpl. Taylor and I had no idea what, if any, other incriminating evidence would be found until later in the day, when we gathered at the detachment for a full briefing with all members involved in the investigation.

Another major break. Guy Butt was wearing all of his clothes when we apprehended him, which meant we didn't have to go looking for them. All was secured at the detachment exhibit room, and the key was turned over to me. For that reason, I could swear under oath, in court, to every exhibit's continuity. Mr. Butt was given a standard full-length jumpsuit to wear with slippers.

In all investigations that eventually end up in court, the fewer people involved, the better. Later, the seized exhibits would be properly marked, bagged, and forwarded to the RCMP lab in Sackville, NB, for forensic examination. The police science lab had the latest equipment to test for what we asked them. After testing, the examiner (only one) would record the results for their personal file. He or she would re-secure the exhibit and forward it back to the sending member. From there to the original security locker, and it would stay that way until presented in court, where it would be opened. Of course, the examining personnel, most of whom are civilian members, would also have to give evidence as to his or her findings and the continuity of the exhibit. It all came down to facts and evidence: how it was gathered, how it was preserved, and how it was presented. The judge, or judge and jury, made the final decision of guilt or innocence. In those days, a statement of admission, after police caution, was usually the icing on the cake.

Again and again, without any of us even saying a word, Mr. Butt talked about where he was, what he did, where he had gone, how he was loaded on beer and drugs, how he had left his friend's house and had to clear his head and sober up before he went home to his wife. He talked about how he walked the road, past the murder scene, a route he had taken hundreds of times before. He didn't see or hear anything. When his head cleared enough to go home, he walked to his boat on the slipway, just to make sure it was secure, and sat and had a smoke or two.

"So, why go there?" I asked.

"The locals are always on the beach, especially in winter. They shoot birds from the shore. I wanted to make sure everything was the way I left it, that's all. I have done this many times. That boat is all I got to go birding with. If something happens to it, I'm fucked. Hey, if I had found anything out of place, I would be the first one to call the cops. Hey, man, I had problems here before, which no one did anything about. Someone got the boat to the water and left it there. I called and you did nothing to find out who fucked with it."

As planned, we let him ramble. I was the note taker. I never spoke to him directly. If he spoke to me directly, I always answered with one syllable: yes, no, or what. Cpl. Taylor did all the talking.

Head down, never looking at either of us. He rambled on and on. To me, it seemed like he was trying to convince himself that he hadn't done anything. However, there was one piece of evidence that he would never be able to explain. It was obvious that he was coming down from the high he had, and I knew he must be hurting physically.

He didn't say anything we were interested in hearing. We

just listened. When Sol asked a question, he had all the right answers. Nothing he said either helped us or implicated him.

By 9:30 a.m. he still hadn't said anything useful. I looked at the clock and thought I should be home, mine a lot different than his. His was a small cell, 6 x 14, with a double steel bunk and foam mattresses, toilet, and steel faucet. We drank coffee after coffee.

"Guy, if you're hungry, I can get you something to eat. If not, maybe a coffee."

He spoke directly to me for the first time.

"What's your name again?"

This time it wasn't Cst. Gruchy. This time it was Tom. "My name is Tom. Can I get you anything?"

He said he would kill for a smoke, so I passed him one and lit it. "How about something to eat?" I asked again.

"Nah, I'm not hungry, but a coffee would be great."

"No problem."

Time was crucial. We stuck to our plan. I was to be his very best friend—the good cop. Cpl. Taylor was the other fellow—the bad cop. I was the gofer, and Sol was the interviewer. I wasn't to initiate any conversation, but I was to answer direct questions and more or less tend on him. It was important that he could rely on me and trust me. It was important that he think of me as a cop. I also had to make sure all conversations were recorded accurately, verbatim.

When Sol left the room, we would just engage in general conversation, nothing about the crime. When he asked for something reasonable, and I could get it, I made sure he got it: cigarettes, coffee, food.

"Guy, want to take a shower?" We had one in the back.

"Fuck, a shower would be great."

Afterwards, I could tell that he felt a lot better.

"That coffee would be good. No problem, hey Tom?" My first name, a major breakthrough. "Any chance of another smoke?"

As required by law, within three days of a warrant's being issued, the suspect had to be brought before a judge or magistrate, not a Justice of the Peace. The Crown would ask for a mental assessment, usually thirty days at the Waterford Hospital in St. John's. The court usually ordered it anyway, and it was definitely in the suspect's best interests. That would be Monday. Today, Saturday, we still had a lot of blanks to fill in. Guy was advised that he could speak to a lawyer without delay, but he didn't ask for one. Another plus. At his first court hearing, through his lawyer, court-appointed or otherwise, the chances were that he would be remanded in custody for a psychiatric evaluation, and from there a bail hearing. All this would be the sole decision of the judge after hearing a brief summary of the facts from both sides.

I returned with coffee and cigarettes. I even gave him a full package of smokes, his brand. It was imperative that I win his confidence. He had to believe that I was his very best friend and confidant. He had to trust me.

From the time he was arrested, three and a half days before his first court appearance, he didn't ask for a lawyer. I allowed him to see his immediate family, and I was always present. Each time, I advised him that he was still under caution and that anything he said could be used against him in court. For court purposes, if the case went to trial, the less outside involvement from other policemen, the better.

The interview process over the next couple of days was not overly stressful on anyone. It was always short and to the point. Cpl. Taylor and I were the only RCMP members who talked to the suspect. His first whole day and night in custody, I interrupted the second interview, which was planned, by asking him how his family was holding up. One word: "Okay."

Out of the blue, while talking to Sol, he asked me, "Tom, how about a Coke?"

I returned with the soft drink and an apple flip. "Here, thought you might be a little hungry."

"Yeah, thanks."

I sat in the background and continued to take notes.

In the meantime, all his clothing was being hand-delivered to the police laboratory services in New Brunswick. They could easily examine it for things invisible to the naked eye and prepare everything found to be presented in court for the Crown.

"Tom, any chance in seeing the missus this evening?"

"I'll give her a call later and let you know."

Things were moving slowly, but at least they were moving forward. I left to make the call, and I made eye contact with my partner upon my return. He asked me how I made out.

"Good. Guy, seven thirty."

"Thanks."

This interview lasted an hour and forty-three minutes. He was returned to the holding cell and waited for supper.

After a very short meeting, Cpl. Taylor returned to St. John's. He would be back tomorrow, same time, same place. I got Mr. Butt something to eat and sat outside the cell. Neither of us spoke, and I was okay with that. He was very anxious to see his wife. This would be the first time since he was arrested. A female matron would search her. Not a strip search, but in private, and other than that, without exception I would always be present. She could talk about whatever she wanted, even the matter under investigation. She was never coached. Everything had to be voluntary. Anything that he might say to her that was relevant to the investigation could still be used against him.

Guy's wife arrived right on time. I allowed them half an hour. She cried a lot. Neither of them said very much. There were long minutes of deafening silence, then *how's Mom, how's Dad*, that sort of thing. I gave them an extra fifteen minutes or so. I never had to ask her to leave—she suddenly stood up, he kissed her, then she looked at me and said, "Thanks." The matron, who remained in the back, showed her out, and I returned him to the cell.

"Gotta go, Guy. You've eaten, I haven't, and I'm starved."

"Here, have some of mine."

"Like to, but no thanks. I have beans and wieners waiting at home." He laughed, and so did I. "See you in the morning. By the way, want something to read?"

"Nah. Hey, thanks, Tom."

"No sweat."

We were scheduled to get the preliminary results from the lab the next day. The exhibits would have been analyzed, the findings could change everything. Maybe get an admission of guilt. Anything would be better than what we had up to that point. It was important that he tell us what he knew before court. I was getting pissed off. My patience was growing thin, but I had to play the game.

"Your wife called a few minutes ago and wants to drop by this afternoon. It's up to you." Cpl. Taylor was aware of this before we sat down and knew that I was going to mention it.

"What time will she be here? Same as last time?"

I lied and told him that the afternoon was no good for the matron. We were under no obligation to let him have any visitors. In a larger area, St. John's, for example, he probably wouldn't have gotten any visitors, but we relaxed the rules a little.

"Yeah, that's great." He looked at me, and this time I felt that he was sincere. "Thanks, Tom."

"I'll call later to confirm."

I felt that this would give him something to look forward to, and maybe there would be a change in his attitude during the interview. With notebook in hand and back on my perch, the show went on. Nothing happened that would be of any consequence, at least not yet. We had another staff meeting, and after five, we wrapped everything up until the morning.

When I called his wife, she answered the phone. Everything was set for seven thirty. She asked if she could bring him his supper. She had fried fish and mashed potatoes, his favourite. I told her it wasn't necessary, but she really wanted to cook a meal for him. At this point, she fully believed in his innocence. She was his wife, and she loved him and would stand by him, for better or for worse. She was a very young woman, and most would say very foolish.

"Tom, there's no way he did this. Not him. I know he's far from perfect, but I do know the man I married." Did she? She was convinced of his innocence. What she had heard around the community, no way, it just wasn't possible. "Please, just this one time. I won't ask for anything else, I promise."

I understood where she was coming from. Without thinking about it anymore, and figuring I could use it to my advantage, I agreed. "Just this once. Remember, I trust you, and I'll be there."

"I know. Thanks. I could bring some extra for you if you would like."

"I would love that," I lied, "but I don't think the rest of the members would appreciate it."

Meekly, she said, "I understand," then laughed.

I couldn't accept her offer, even if I wanted to, but it was a kind gesture all the same.

"Guy, the missus is bringing in your supper. Supposed to be your favourite."

I didn't tell him what it was, and he didn't ask. I couldn't get over the look on his face. I thought his eyes filled up, but I couldn't be sure, as he turned toward the bunk and sat down. He asked for a cigarette, and I offered him the last one in my pack. I insisted and said, "I'll pick up more on the way back tonight. See you at around seven."

"Yeah."

In the grand scheme of things, I believed it was working. I was sure of it. It had to—time was getting short. I was also liked by his immediate family. I had nothing against them. They would surely pay a heavy price, but it was his fault, not theirs. I continued to see the victim's face and how he had punished her before killing her.

The lab report came in while he was enjoying his fish and potatoes. Blood samples on his clothing and his boots matched the victim's. That made my day, even though it didn't come as a surprise. The boot prints had not been analyzed by the lab. They were handled by our St. John's Ident Section. We knew we had a match to the prints left at the scene, around the slipway, and at the doorstep. Everything was starting to add up.

I let him have an extra-long visit with his wife. I was still hoping that there was a chance, no matter how slim, he would give us an admission of guilt. It didn't look good. Tomorrow was our last chance to get a statement, and we only had part of the day. At three o'clock he had to be arraigned before a magistrate in Harbour Grace. I had no doubt that he would be remanded to the Waterford Hospital. I sat and talked with him while waiting for the on-duty guard, whom I had told not to come in until nine thirty. I just wanted to hang around a bit after his wife had left and have a little chat. Nothing about the file, unless, of course, he volunteered something. We just talked.

Three days in a cell might seem like a lifetime to some, especially with something as serious as a murder charge hanging over their heads. This was the first time he had been locked up. I could understand why he wanted me to hang around. I didn't mind. The more relaxed and comfortable he was with me, the better.

The day after tomorrow, while he was in remand, I would be able to get back to a regular routine and devote all my time on the follow-up to the investigation. I wouldn't be assigned any other files while I was working on this one.

We had a coffee and a couple of smokes together. He was on one side of the locked cell door, and I was on the other. The outside doorbell rang.

"That's your guard for this evening."

As I stood up, I could hear him say, "Yeah, fuck it."

In the prisoner's presence, I reminded everyone of the rules so there would be no misunderstanding: no talking between guard and prisoner.

"Guy, if you want a coffee, soft drink, or water, fine, but sorry, as in the last couple of nights, no smoking."

Both prisoner and guard indicated that they understood. It was the same guard we used the previous two nights, but I had to go through this routine each time I left for the evening.

"Guy, if anything comes up and you need to talk to me about why you're here, the guard has my number."

That was the first and only thing I mentioned about the incident, and which I had also said the two previous nights. I hoped he would tell me what had happened, but he never said a word about it. His wife hadn't left yet, and I heard her tell him that she loved him.

"Guy, tell the truth. You didn't do that to that woman, did you?"

"No way. I didn't, I swear! I don't know anything about it, and I don't know why they have me locked up. I swear to God, I never done nothing, you got to believe me."

She didn't answer. As she left, she turned and looked at him and said, "I love you. Good night. Tom, can I drop by tomorrow?"

"I don't think that's going to be possible, as we have to be in Harbour Grace court at three. I'll let you know. It depends."

I said this in the hopes that he might tell me what I wanted to hear, on the off chance that he could see his wife before going to court. She shook my hand.

"I understand. Thanks."

I could tell she was hurting. It was obvious by now that she knew a lot more than she was letting on. Living in a small community as she did. Everyone knowing just about everything that goes on. She probably knew what I and everyone else knew. She looked me in the eyes, and for the first time I could see that her eyes were full of tears.

"I do love him."

I just answered by saying, "Good night. See what happens tomorrow." I felt sorry for her.

When she was gone, Guy asked, "Is she okay?"

"I guess as good as can be expected, considering."

"Yeah. See you in the morning."

As I turned to walk away, he said, "Tom."

"Yeah?"

"Never mind."

Without thinking, I said, "See you in the morning, God willing."

As I walked to my car, I thought about how much I really loathed that man, and one side of me was relieved that I wouldn't have to deal with him in any way for at least the next month or so. I had myself convinced that I wasn't going to think about it anymore until tomorrow. Home, something to eat, a few drinks, and off to bed.

I was dog-tired when I hit the pillow at midnight, but I never slept a wink all night. I watched the clock hour after hour. It appeared to move in slow motion, but my mind was like an express train, rehashing everything, wondering what I had left out, what else I could do to get him to admit to the murder. At 6:45 a.m., I couldn't lie in bed any longer. My family knew what I was going through, and I loved them for the way they were handling it. It was also very hard on them.

I dressed and told my wife I was going in early. I might as well, I said, as I was keeping her awake. It was cold outside, but not nearly as cold as it had been just a couple of days earlier. This was a refreshing kind of cold for someone who hadn't slept a wink. This was probably going to be the longest day of all: court in Harbour Grace for sure, and a trip to the Waterford Hospital with him. I had my mind made up, though, that it wouldn't be me taking him into town. When he left that courthouse, I didn't want to lay eyes on him for at least a month.

I enjoyed the slow drive up the shore to the highway. I met the odd vehicle on the way and wondered what their occupants were up to. I dropped into the Trans-Canada Highway Irving for a coffee. I wasn't in any kind of hurry. When I got to the detachment at 8:15 a.m., he was asleep. For a second I wished I were so lucky. I couldn't imagine how he could sleep at all with what he had on his mind, yet I was the one getting stressed out.

The guard was reading a book. I whispered, "Good morning. If he's not awake by nine, I'll call him," and went to my desk. I figured I had an hour or so to catch up on some long-overdue paperwork. I ordered his breakfast from the Irving for 9:15. Cpl. Taylor would be here from town around ten o'clock for our last try at getting a statement. By this time I had all but given up on any chance of that happening.

Cpl. Taylor walked in right on time. I filled him in on the night before.

"Nothing new."

"Okay. You keep up exactly what you're doing. Me, no more Mr. Nice Guy. This morning the shit hits the fan. You'll see what I mean as we go along. One thing's for certain: he'll know I'm really pissed off with him. Before the morning is over, he'll know exactly what we have on him, and he'll have to see how useless it is for him to keep up with the bullshit. That's about it. There is nothing more either of us can do. Let's go see what happens." I laughed, even though I didn't feel very happy.

We both entered the interview room as usual. I felt the tension, knowing the way this interview would go.

"Morning," I said. He answered with the same, and that was it. The next thing I heard startled me.

"Okay, sit the fuck down."

The accused was as surprised as I was. "Tom, what time are we leaving for Harbour Grace?"

"Close to one. We don't want to hang around the court-house, waiting."

Cpl. Taylor snapped, "Don't you worry about the court-house. You'll get there when we're good and ready, and not before." I will never forget the way they both stared at each other. "Now sit there, shut up, and listen. Believe it or not, I am going to do you a big favour. Here's the way it is."

Like the professional he was, Sol started from the beginning and went over most of the evidence we had against him. Guy didn't move. His head was down, his gaze fixed on the floor. He never said a word, just sat nervously on his hands and listened. He looked my way, briefly.

"Don't look at him. It's me you have to be concerned with now."

"All right, b'y, don't have a heart attack. What the fuck? Tom, how about a smoke?"

"Are you deaf? What did I just tell you? Give him nothing! You look and talk to me, not him, understand? Like I said, I'm the one you should be concerned with. I have absolutely no time for you or your kind. You know what you are. I can't think of a word that would be even close to describing the kind of person you are. You know exactly how this went down, and now you know that we do. Now's the time. Be a man, think about your family, stop with the bullshit, make life easier for everybody. Think about your family. Your wife, your mother, your father, man. You're going down, and you know it."

I couldn't believe the sudden shift in Sol's interview technique. *God, I really hope this works.* There was a long silence. No one moved. Not a word was spoken. Then, without warning, Cpl. Taylor stood up, knocking the chair over in the process. He looked at me.

"Got to make a phone call. Be right back."

What was he doing? What did he want me to do? After the door closed, I stayed exactly where I was.

"Fuck, man, who pissed on his cornflakes?"

Guy asked me for a cigarette. Out of habit, and without thinking, I gave him one.

"What's with him?"

"Hey, I'm just as surprised as you are."

"Will the wife be there this afternoon?"

"Most likely. I'm not sure. I don't think you'll get much of a chance to talk to her, even if she is."

"I'm not even sure if I want her to be there."

"I'll call her for you and let her know if you would rather she wasn't there."

"Don't bother. Whatever happens happens."

I gave him a second cigarette. He was very agitated, maybe because of the way the interview was going, or maybe because of his pending court hearing. He didn't say, and I didn't ask.

I heard myself say, "Look, forget it, you're probably right. Maybe he's pissed off with making all these trips from St. John's. It is a weekend, remember."

"Yeah, fuck him."

Cpl. Taylor was out of the room for about ten minutes, and when he returned, it started all over again. The suspect didn't say a word, just looked at the floor, the wall, the ceiling—anything at all but Taylor.

"Eleven fifty-five, what time do I eat?"

"When I say you can. What did I tell you about talking to him?" A few minutes later, Sol said, "Tom, get him something to eat. I have a few things to take care of."

Food was again ordered from the Irving and delivered to the detachment. Mr. Butt and I were alone all through his dinner. We never spoke. He looked at me several times, and we made eye contact. I felt for sure that after this session there would be no hope for a confession. Precious time wasted. The good news was that we had enough evidence to prove his guilt. At least, I hoped we did.

He ate everything without saying a word. I couldn't help but notice by his facial expressions and his mannerisms that he was on edge and concerned. He asked for another cigarette, and I threw the half-pack on the desk.

"Here, help yourself. Now all you'll need is a light."

"I'll owe you a case before this is all over. I really hope the wife will be there. Maybe you'll let me see her for a couple of minutes."

"We'll see how it goes, but I can't make any promises."

"I know."

"Where's that other prick?"

"I have no idea. Probably in the outside office. Do you want to talk to him?"

"Fuck, no. He's just a prick."

I had seen Cpl. Sol Taylor in action before. He was one of the best in the Force. There was no sign of him by 12:35. Guy smoked two or three cigarettes right after each other. I watched the large clock on the wall behind him tick, tick, ticking away. It would soon be time to leave. I was tired, and I was finding it hard to concentrate. And I still had to go to Harbour Grace.

"Tom, thanks for everything."

Hey, no problem, I almost said, *what are friends for?* I had a little chuckle to myself. More silence, another couple of cigarettes.

"I would really like to talk to the wife."

"Like I said, Guy, if there is any way I can let you, I will. You have my word." And I meant it.

Around 12:45, he turned several times just to look at the clock. I felt like a warden watching a prisoner on death row—a prisoner looking at his last moments on earth. What he didn't know was that court was actually at three o'clock, not two. We had to have that extra hour, just in case.

CHAPTER 7
THE CONFESSION

"Tom."

"Yeah?"

He was sitting across from me with his head down and a cigarette in his hand. The silence was deafening.

"What is it, Guy? Want something?"

I remember this as if it were today.

"I did it. I killed her. I don't know what the fuck came over me, but I did it. I got to tell someone."

My heart sank, and I felt weak. I couldn't believe what I had just heard.

"Guy, you know you are under caution and that you don't have to say anything."

"I know. I did it," he repeated. "I was drinking all day. Fuck, I must have had two dozen beer at my buddy's house. We started seven or eight in the morning. There was this young girl there. We knew each other. She was a friend of my buddy's daughter. The more I drank, the more I wanted her. I wasn't thinking clearly, all that booze. All I knew was that I was going to have her. As the day went on, the more I drank, the more I was going to have her. I knew when and where. She was young, about sixteen, a good-looking girl, long red hair. She was there all day and evening. I knew who she was, where she lived, and she knew who I was, too. I also knew which way she would go when she went home, the same way she always did when it was late. Her house was only about ten minutes away at the most, just down the path, up the road, around the bend, and home.

"The more I drank, the more I planned. There was a shortcut right behind the house, up over a small hill that cut off the long bend in the road. Just a minute or two and you're at the main road and ahead of the curve. A lot of people use it, but rarely late at night. I used it many times. It's well-used with a well-beaten path. I knew she would walk the road. As soon as she left to go home, so did I. I wasn't thinking about anything else, none of the consequences, nothing, just her. I hid, waiting for her to come by. She walked up the guardrail side of the road. At the right spot I ran across the road and tackled her. She never saw me coming. She never even glanced around. We both fell over the guardrail. I had the hood tightened on the snowsuit; all you could see was my eyes. I wanted her, and I was going to have her, and that was it. I didn't think of anything else. Sex, just sex, that was all, nothing else."

Guy continued, and he said that he was sorry over and over again. He kept talking, and I kept listening. He was like someone in a hypnotic trance. I knew exactly how important this was, and I recorded everything. Our efforts had paid off tenfold.

"I landed on top of her, and she went face down in the snow. I turned her over. Jesus, I couldn't believe it. I couldn't believe what I was seeing. It wasn't her. It was an older woman, and I didn't even know her. I was sitting across her and had my hand over her mouth. I saw someone walk up the road on the same side I was hiding. It was her. I watched as she walked past us up the road and home. I was totally fucked up. I never had a clue what had happened. I panicked. I had no fucking idea who this woman was. It was like I was having a dream or something."

He wanted to talk, and I was more than happy to just listen. We had what we wanted.

"I hit her hard, really hard, over and over. I couldn't stop. I just kept hitting her with my fists, and I couldn't stop. I was angry. I hit her again and again. She cried and cried. I put my hand over her mouth and told her to shut the fuck up. I had my mind made up. She wore a two-piece snowsuit, and it didn't take much to pull down the pants. I told her to shut the fuck up, don't make a fucking sound. I tried, but I couldn't get into her. Everything was happening too fast. I remember she called me by name—somehow she knew me. She said that there was no one at home at her house and that we could go there and I could do what I want. She said her husband had died a while ago and she was alone. I think she said he had cancer. She knew me. She said she did. Now what? I was all fucked up. I remember standing up, and she was on her back in the snow. I didn't feel anything. She was naked, lying in the snow, and I didn't feel a thing, fuck all. I kicked her in the head. I remember seeing her false teeth fly in the air and across the road. She was more or less whimpering all the time. I was really scared and didn't know what to do, just like in a dream. I'm not like that. I never hurt anyone like this. Fuck."

The door to the interview room opened, and he stopped talking. The expression on his face told me everything. He hated my partner, and maybe for good reason. I was the one he trusted—I was his friend. I stood. Cpl. Taylor took one look at me and closed the door. He knew, and I knew he knew. Guy asked me about seeing his wife in Harbour Grace, and I gave him the same answer as before. No promises. However, I did know that I would try my best for them to have a few minutes together.

My very first question, to keep the conversation going after the interruption, was, "Tell me, Guy, what happened after you kicked her?"

He took several deep draws on his cigarette with his head down.

"What the fuck, it's over for me. The booze, the fucking booze. I was really pissed off. What the fuck was she doing here anyway, an old woman? I was waiting for someone else, not her. I beat her up, kicked her, tried to rape her. I knew I was in deep shit. Everything was happening so fast. No one saw me. There was no one else around, not a soul. I knew what I had to do. I didn't have any choice. I knew where I was and had no idea who she was, but she knew me. Don't know why—I just kept hitting her in the face, over and over. She was moaning, and I just wanted her to stop and be quiet. She did for a bit but then started again.

"Fuck, Tom, I didn't mean any of this. I just couldn't stop. The more she moaned, the more I hit her. Finally, nothing. I was sitting across her and she never moved. Quiet. I got off and sat next to her. There was blood everywhere. I didn't rape her. I was going to, but I couldn't. Probably all the beer and whatever. I cleaned my face and hands in the snow. I never moved. I was really scared. Without thinking, I turned her over, face down, and dragged her toward the edge of the cliff. I had my mind made up. I knew what I had to do. I didn't think about anything else. I thought that no one would ever know."

He continued to smoke cigarette after cigarette, and I lit them for him. No time to stop now. Let him hang himself. He looked right at me, and this time his eyes were full of tears. For a fleeting moment I felt sorry for him.

"Jesus, Tom. Fuck, man, I'm sorry. What can I do? What about the wife, my mother, father, my sister? I swear that's it for me, I'll never drink again, I swear to God."

I had to keep going while he wanted to talk. I had to know everything. Some questions I didn't want to ask, but I had to. My hair stood on end. He was a sadistic bastard—a killer—sitting just three feet from me, smoking my cigarettes. I was running errands for him, serving him his meals, getting what he wanted, and he thought I was his friend. He had forgotten that I was a police officer.

Again I asked, "Then what happened?"

He looked directly into my eyes. His were very heavy, like those of a whipped puppy. It didn't bother me. The more I thought he hurt, the better I felt. I didn't really give a damn about him. Three days without booze? This was probably the longest time he had been sober. Despite that, I somehow got the feeling that he was relieved. The smoke from the cigarettes filled the room.

"She started moaning, real low, not near loud enough for anyone up on the road to hear her, a low, continuous moan. I had her by her ankles, and she was face down with her arms up above her head and hands outstretched. She wasn't fighting. She wasn't doing anything. I knew where I was and where the edge of the cliff was. I had no choice. She saw me and knew who I was. I was going to throw her over, and she'd be gone. No one would find her. If they did find her sometime, there would be no way to say what happened to her.

"I got to the edge and picked her up. She didn't weigh very much. I had no trouble getting her on my shoulder. She didn't move. I thought she was dead. Without thinking, I just threw her over the bank to the ocean below. I looked over the edge, and there she was. She hit the rocks and didn't land in the water. I didn't heave her far enough. What time is it? What about court? What about the wife? She is going to be wondering where we are."

"No worries," I lied. "We contacted the court clerk, and they're running late, and we have to be there by three. We called your wife. Guy, you said you were mad after you threw her over the bank. How come? What made you so upset?"

"I looked over the bank, and I saw her on the rocks. I wasn't sure she was dead. She landed on the cliff about twenty, thirty feet down, and not in the water, like I wanted. I knew that cliff was there, but I didn't think about it. I was sure someone would find her. I had to move her, and I couldn't just leave her there like that. Sooner or later, someone would come across her. If she was in the water, she would probably never be found. I thought about my boat on the slipway, down by the house. I could handle it. There would be no one around to see me. I'd put the boat out, row around the point, and haul her off the rocks into the water. It was a very short distance from my boat to where she was, a couple of minutes at the most. I knew there would be no trouble hauling her off the rocks. I couldn't get the boat off the slipway. It was froze on. I went home and went to bed. I was going back in the morning to get the boat off. I'm really fucked, ain't I?"

I didn't answer—I felt sad, and I felt elated. I still had a question to which I needed to know the answer, but that could wait. Not here, not now. I'd know when the time was right. It had to be today, because after court I probably wouldn't get the chance. We left the interview room, and he went back to the cell.

We were all in the main office. I walked in, and all eyes were on me. I didn't say much, just asked what time were we leaving for court. No one spoke.

"Anyone want a coffee?"

I went to the coffee pot, as casual as could be, grabbed a cup, then turned and looked at everyone.

"We got the bastard. Everything. Here it is."

What a transformation in a room!

"Sarge, I've got a shock for everyone. She wasn't the one that he planned to attack. She wasn't the intended victim." You could hear a pin drop. "That's right. He was waiting for someone else, and that someone else walked right by them, on the other side of the road, just a couple of minutes later, and apparently never saw or heard a thing. They were just a couple hundred yards away from each other, but because of that ninety-degree bend in the road, they wouldn't have been able to see each other."

What were the odds? Two women out alone on a bitterly cold March night, walking home, and each totally unaware of the other's existence. Just a few minutes either way and they probably would have met each other and walked home safely together. But it wasn't meant to be. One of the two was never going home again. She was at the wrong place at the wrong time.

All told, he had killed the wrong woman. If not for Paul's confession, we probably would never have known anything about the other person. It certainly didn't change anything as far as the victim was concerned, but it did mean that we would have to talk to her. How was she going to react? And how about her parents? A very, very lucky young lady. She had absolutely no idea how close she had come to dying at the hands of this man.

CHAPTER 8
FIRST APPEARANCE

After the briefing, and after everyone had been brought up to speed, we planned our trip to Harbour Grace. All hands were very pleased, to say the least—a team effort that had gone very well. But there was no time to celebrate. There was still a load of work to do. I wanted to drive Guy in a marked police car alone. There were a couple of things I had to know, just for my own information. Two members, Cpl. Taylor and a uniformed police officer from St. John's, would escort him to town afterwards. They would follow me to court in an unmarked car.

I was relieved. I didn't have to think about going to St. John's with him. By this time I'd had enough of him to last me a lifetime. I really did have a need to get away from him. When we left the detachment, he was in the back seat with the silent patrolman up and secured. This is a bulletproof cage made of Plexiglas and encased in steel, which extends from doorpost to doorpost and from the top of the back of the front seat to the roof. This gives the driver total protection from anyone in the back of the cruiser.

"Do you think the wife will still be there?"

"I'm sure she will," I answered, without knowing one way or the other. To be honest, I didn't care.

"Can I have a smoke?"

"Sorry, don't have any," I lied.

For obvious reasons, he couldn't smoke in the back of the car, anyway. My mind was racing, which seemed to be the routine for me lately. I was feeling tired, most likely from lack of sleep and frustration. I constantly checked on him by looking in the rear-view mirror. He was okay. The road was packed with snow and patches of what looked like pure ice with gravel underneath. There was very little pavement on the Tilton Barrens back then. Several times I felt the back of the car sway a little. I wasn't doing anywhere near the posted speed limit of fifty miles per hour. I was driving as the road conditions dictated. We had lots of time. I was in complete control.

Faith and a lot of luck, if you believe in either, gave a young girl a second chance, a chance to grow up, to love and be loved, a chance to experience life at its fullest, a chance to raise a family, see the stars, the moon and the sun, with eyes full of life, not like the victim, who had been found looking at the sky, the stars, and the moon but seeing nothing.

I am writing this nearly three decades later, for the victim, her family, and myself, something that I feel has to be done. If not, besides those mentioned, who will remember? I have never met the lady in real life, but she has been part of my life ever since I found her. I will never forget her eyes staring at me. I need closure, as do her family, although I really don't expect that to happen.

I remember having to break the news to her family, with whom she had spent the last few hours of her life. It wasn't only Mrs. Callan who died way back then. A large part of the extended family she left so abruptly also died in one way or another.

"Hi, I'm Cst. Gruchy. Would you be Phyllis Head?"

I will never forget the look of helplessness on her daughter's face, a look of instant despair. It was too much for her to take in all at once. A pretty face now distorted by pain. There was no humanly way possible for her to stop the tears.

"Why?" Over and over again. "Why my mother? She never hurt anyone in her whole life. Why her?"

I couldn't say anything. The questions came one after another. I couldn't answer then, but I promised her I would, and very soon. I left that family in total despair, shock, and disbelief, and I couldn't do anything about it. Absolutely nothing.

As I was driving, based on all the facts, I could see exactly what happened. I could picture her walking up the road, around the corner, and on the way home. I couldn't possibly know what she was thinking. This lady had been through so much. She cared for a husband she loved with all her heart and soul, until cancer took him from her at a very young age, just a couple of years earlier. This lady loved her family more than life itself. Her death and the way she died left a lasting impression on me and everyone who knew her. I'm a stranger, not related, but rest assured that her memory will remain with me in my heart and in my mind for as long as I live. Family, friends, and neighbours, they will also never forget. It hurts. Mrs. Callan should never be forgotten, and if I have anything to say about it, she won't.

In life she was more than blessed to have what she had: a loving husband, three sons, three daughters, and loving grandchildren. Maybe that's what she was thinking about as she walked home. I would like to think so—no fear, warm in her winter clothing, not a worry. That night would be different; she wouldn't see her home ever again. Her daughter wouldn't get the usual expected call that she was safe. Phyllis would be contacted, all right, but not in the way she wanted. I, a stranger, a police officer, would be talking to her with news that no one wants to hear. A loved one gone, not only dead, but murdered. Life for the family, as they knew it, would never be the same again.

Was there a lesson to be learned? Of course there was, sad as it is to say. Never walk alone. It wasn't safe or wise even then, and for sure it's not safe now. Bad things should never happen to good people, but unfortunately they do. They did in 1986, and will again in 2018 and beyond. She was innocent and helpless as she walked home. Her fate was already decided. Mrs. Minnie Callan, widow, mother, and grandmother, was going to die. Her destiny was decided long before she left her daughter's house in Long Cove.

Guy Butt was angry. Why? He had attacked the wrong person. The one he really wanted was home and out of harm's way, safe and sound. From the start, when he left the house and took the shortcut up over the hill, he had planned to attack a young woman. He killed Mrs. Callan instead, and for no other reason than to save his own skin.

After being with him for those few days, I knew him much better than he thought I did. Why did he beat her the way he did? Anger and frustration, hours of planning gone down the drain. No more to it than that. I had no control over what happened to him from here on. I wished I did. I wished I was his judge and jury. One thing I could do, though, was to make certain he paid for what he did. I couldn't decide his fate, but I could damn well make sure that he was brought before people who could.

As we drove along, he said sorry, sorry, sorry, over and over again, just words without meaning, no soul to them. My mother came to mind. *Crocodile tears*, she would say, and that's exactly what they were. Was I hard-hearted? You bet I was. He could say he was sorry until he was blue in the face, or until the cows came home, but nothing he or anyone else could say would bring Minnie Callan back to her family, where she belonged.

I couldn't help but wonder how sorry he would be if he had never gotten caught. Saying you're sorry means nothing unless it comes from the heart. Now he was saying he was sorry he had killed her—but more likely he was sorry he was in the back of a police car on the way to court.

"Tom, honest to God, I didn't mean it."

What bullshit. There were, however, two sides to Guy Butt. I saw both, the man and the killer. I lived with him for three days, and I didn't much like either one. Off and on, as we drove along, I thought I understood where one side was coming from, and I could probably live with it if I had to. The other side I despised. I wondered if he felt the same way about himself.

Road conditions were far from being ideal. God blessed us

with no snow—not a flake since Thursday night—cold for sure. I could live with cold. I didn't have to shovel it, and it didn't shag up the crime scene.

I drove with care and caution, slowly but surely. I had driven across the barrens hundreds of times before. It cut off more than an hour away from Whitbourne to the mall in Carbonear. Driving didn't bother me in the least, no matter what the conditions. I was in no hurry. Time was on my side. I had lots of time to think, of which I took good advantage. I was content in knowing, God willing, that tonight I was going home, and Guy Butt wasn't.

He would tell me what I wanted to know. I was sure of it. If not, no visit with family. It was one or the other. Before he stepped one foot out of the car, I would know, even though I was scared to hear what he had to say. Soon I would be free of him, at least for a while. I had a lot of follow-up work to do, and he would only cross my mind when he absolutely had to.

I hadn't had a good night's sleep since Thursday. No wonder I felt the way I did. For three days my mind had been in overdrive. Not sleeping or eating right wasn't good for anyone.

Harbour Grace was the point of no return. Now was the time. I thought about Phyllis. The look on her face was haunting me, as was her mom's. The family had no idea how this case bothered me. Guy Butt's faith was in the hands of justice. Mrs. Callan died on March 13, one day after my oldest daughter's birthday.

"Tom, Tom." As if from a distance. I was lost in thought. "Tom!"

"What? What is it?" For a second, he startled me.

"Do you think the wife will be there?"

"Guy, I told you over and over again, I have no idea. I would say she will. I told her on the phone exactly what was going on, when court was, and that's all I can do."

"Thanks. Are you sure I can't have a smoke?"

I didn't want to shut him down, not this close. If his wife was there, which I felt confident she would be, I'd ask him before I let him out of the car. Like I said, no answer, no visit. It was as simple as that. My last chance, but for sure the best time to get to the truth. Everything he had said before didn't really bother me much, but now every word he spoke was cutting through me like a dull knife. I just had to have a smoke.

I stopped over halfway across the barrens, got out, and spoke to the other officers following me. I went back to the car and let him out. I needed a cigarette just as badly as he did, if not more.

"Here." I lit his first. Why I stopped, I have no idea. I just did. Why I gave him another cigarette, I have no idea. Here we were, four cops, one in uniform and three not, stopped on the New Harbour Barrens a little after 2:30 p.m., smoking cigarettes, Guy leaning back against the rear quarter panel on the driver's side, and me right next to him. No cuffs. Where could he go?

The officers in the ghost car must have thought I was crazy. They didn't say anything, but I didn't care one way or another. We never said a word, me and my buddy. Just standing there having a smoke. What could be better than this? It was probably the best cigarette I'd ever had, if there is such a thing. It was great—just me, the cigarette, and the killer. What more could anybody want? I laughed to myself. What a joke. Everything was happening much too fast. My mind could barely keep up. Standing next to a killer?

I heard a horn. Time to go. I waved, got back in the car, and off we went. I made my mind up that for the next fifteen miles or so I wasn't going to talk to him. I would ask him when we were on the parking lot. Time was getting short, and I hoped his wife would be waiting for him. If she was, he would be more likely to give me a quick answer without having time to think about it.

On November 15, 2013, I had the pleasure, through a close friend, Elwood Newhook of Norman's Cove, who I first met as a result of this investigation, to speak to Ms. Judy Pinksen, niece of the deceased. I introduced myself, telling her why I called, and we got to know each other over the phone. Now, all those years later, the very same question I needed to ask him came up. I could hardly believe it.

Was she alive when she was thrown over the cliff?

I prayed that she wasn't, but I was scared to hear the truth. I had to know, as did Ms. Pinksen many years later. I could tell her, because he had told me.

We arrived at the Harbour Grace courthouse parking lot. Guy's wife was there, as I expected.

"You okay?"

"Yeah. Can I talk to the wife?"

"Guy, listen. Let's get inside first and we'll see what happens."

"Yeah, okay."

I got out, opened the back door, and cuffed him.

"That favour I asked you about a while back," I said.

"What favour?"

"I need to ask you something, just between you and me".

He was anxious to get out of the car and speak to his wife.

"What is it?"

My heart fluttered in my chest,

"Guy—"

He interrupted again. "I really have to know, what do you think is going to happen?"

I had already told him what to expect. It would only be a few minutes before he would be remanded to the Waterford Hospital, most likely for thirty days.

"Guy." I looked him right in the eye as he sat facing me, half in and half out of the car. "I need the truth. Was she alive when you threw her over the cliff?"

"What do you want to know that for?"

"I have to. Just for me." Everyone was waiting, but no one approached the car. "Was she alive when you threw her over the cliff? Yes or no."

His wife started to walk toward us. Cpl. Taylor stopped her. Thank God. I didn't want any interruptions, not right now.

"Guy?"

"Yeah, she was still alive." No more feeling than that.

"How can you be so sure?"

What he said next tore the heart right out of me.

"She was crying when I threw her over."

Exactly what I hoped I wouldn't hear. It was wishful thinking that she was already dead before she hit the cliff. I was hoping she didn't have to hurt anymore, but it wasn't meant to be. I felt sick. The lady had gone through enough. She knew she was going to die in the worst possible way. Her death was not an easy one. How long was she lying there, naked, before the peace of death took her home? I have convinced myself over the years that this lady died instantly when she hit the jagged rocks.

Minnie Callan, who lived in upper Norman's Cove, was born on June 24, 1925, and died long before her time, murdered on March 13, 1986, just a gunshot away from where she lived. I found it extremely difficult to get a deep breath. At that moment I wished I had never joined the RCMP. A police officer. A peace officer. What did this have to do with peace?

Under normal circumstances, I loved the job that I was trained to do, and I faced all conflict with a stiff upper lip. Forty-eight hundred dollars a year was a lot of money in 1974, when I joined. It was a good wage for a man with a wife and a four-year-old child. Far better than the $27 a week I was making before I joined. As important as the money was, it wasn't why I joined. It was my dream come true. I wanted to feel like I mattered.

As we walked toward the main door, I was holding on to the handcuffs behind his back. I felt content, but not happy. I was content we had this killer in custody and that I had played my part in making it possible, however small it may have been. I knew that when he left Harbour Grace I would have very little, if any, further contact with him. GIS in St. John's would take over. I would, however, have daily contact with all members involved, and we would spend a lot of time together gathering all the relevant evidence and building our file for court. My make-believe friendship with Mr. Butt was history.

Once on the lot, Guy and his wife made a motion to walk toward each other.

"Guy, not here. I told you, let's get inside first."

Cpl. Taylor kept Mrs. Butt occupied. When I gently but firmly pulled Guy back by the cuffs, he looked me right in the eyes. I'm sure that this was the point at which he knew things were different between us.

Sternly, I said, "Guy, I told you, not here on the lot. Wait until we get settled inside. Understand?"

No more best friends. He was the prisoner, and for the first time he knew it.

"You said I could see my wife."

"I said if it was possible, no promises."

Again he said, "You said I could talk to my wife."

"Guy, for fuck's sake, shut up. You're getting on my nerves."

He never said another word about it. I was in charge here, and he knew it. I was, however, going to try my best to let him have a few minutes with his wife. Not for him, but for her. After that he only spoke when spoken to. He was scared that I wouldn't let him see her before he left for St. John's. It felt good. I really liked this side of the fence.

Once inside, Guy and I went to the prisoner's waiting room, which was no bigger than the cell he had been in for the last few days. The big difference was there were no bars. There were two chairs, a small writing table, and one window, about fourteen inches by fourteen, covered with a thick, grey metal screen on the outside. Once inside, I took the cuffs off him. The room itself was maybe ten to fifteen feet directly across from the main door to the only courtroom.

Generally, lawyers used the room to talk to their clients before and after their appearance. Today would be no different. Guy Butt would meet with his lawyer or duty counsel, as the case was here. Duty counsel lawyers were government-appointed at no expense to an accused person. They'd have the opportunity to speak to the accused alone and could take as much time as was necessary to discuss the charge or charges coming before the court and to give advice. In the eyes of the law, everyone, without exception, is treated equally.

Guy would face a magistrate. Magistrates handled the vast majority of criminal offences and all the other statutes. A judge handled the more serious offences. An accused person charged with certain designated offences described in the Criminal Code of Canada as more serious offences, of which murder is one, had the option to be tried by either a judge alone or a judge and jury. The four of us, Mrs. Butt included, waited in the hallway. I was in no hurry, but one thing I was sure of was that I was really looking forward to my ride back home, alone.

His meeting lasted about twenty minutes. From there we all went inside the courtroom. He had to be re-cuffed. Ten minutes later, it was over. The Crown asked for a thirty-day remand to the Waterford Hospital. Duty counsel agreed, and so did His Honour, the magistrate. No plea was taken, and there was no reason not to agree. Such was the case in all extremely serious crimes. The remand was also of great benefit to the accused. He would be assessed by the very best forensic psychiatrists, who would determine if he was in his right mind at the time and fit to stand trial. I was concerned about the final decision, considering the circumstances surrounding the murder. If found not fit, there would be no trial. Simple as that. In thirty days or so, we would know.

Back in the waiting room, Guy Butt was still cuffed, which was how he would stay until he was secured at the Waterford Hospital. We allowed his wife the short visit which he so desperately wanted. The other officers were anxious to get on the road, and I didn't blame them. After all, they had punched in a long day and still had quite a bit to do. Everyone agreed to a ten-minute visit. She came in, and I stood back by the window, where I had a clear view of everything. I motioned to Mrs. Butt to sit in the free chair. Understandably, she looked worried, even a little worn out.

Right away, for the first time, Guy Butt told his wife that he had admitted to everything, that he was drunk and didn't know what he was doing. She didn't answer but started to cry hysterically. They sat across from each other, within touching distance. He reached out and touched her shoulder with his cuffed hands. Calling her by name, repeating over and over how sorry he was. She said nothing, just looked away while sobbing, a river of tears rolling down her face. When she did speak, all she could say was, "Why?" Over and over again. Why?

As we were leaving the room, he kissed her on the cheek and told her he loved her. She whispered, "Me, too."

The officers took over, placed him in the back of the police car, and left for town. He would have his assessments and would then return to Harbour Grace for a bail hearing. I was free of him until then.

CHAPTER 9
BAIL HEARING

The investigation continued, and long hours were punched in by all concerned: GIS Cpl. Solomon Taylor, Ident Sgt. Derek Bishop, K-9 section Max and his master Cpl. Scott Damien, forensics lab in New Brunswick, Sgt. Art Slade (now deceased) in charge of Whitbourne Detachment, all the members of Whitbourne and St. John's detachments, the Whitbourne voluntary fire department, Chief Tom Howe, and me.

There was work to be done. Witnesses had to be interviewed and re-interviewed. The intended victim, the eyewitness, the victim's family, the family of the accused, and many more. Each hour had to be productive. This was a case of immense magnitude, and there was no room for any errors, no matter how minor they seemed to be. We had to be prepared. There were many trips to St. John's for meetings with the chief Crown prosecutor, who would be handling the case. The month seemed to just fly by.

We all appeared in Harbour Grace. The accused was represented by a court-appointed lawyer, and the Waterford Hospital entered their findings into evidence. The report said the accused was fit to stand trial for the charge against him, which was a great relief to all of us. A new date, the following Wednesday, was set for the bail hearing at that time. After submissions from both the Crown and the defence, a decision would be made by the attending magistrate.

The week passed quickly, and we were all back in court for the scheduled bail hearing. Mr. Butt's lawyer did an excellent job in speaking for his client, explaining in full detail all the reasons why the accused should be released on bail. The Crown, on the other hand, adamantly argued against each and every submission of the defence lawyer. He further submitted a brief explaining in intricate detail the reasons why he should remain in custody and backed everything up with specific points of case law (previous evidence accepted as fact in other trials).

Considering the extremely cruel nature of the crime, and the tight-knit community in which it had occurred, I personally didn't think for a minute that the accused would be released on bail. I was right. He wasn't. Guy was remanded back to Her Majesty's Penitentiary in St. John's until his next appearance two weeks down the road, this time for his plea to the charges against him—guilty or not guilty—and his election—whether he wanted to be tried by a Supreme Court judge alone or judge and jury. The only difference this time was that we would all be heading to Brigus, the province's seat for all matters to be heard in District Court (Supreme Court) for the pre-described area which included Norman's Cove, where the murder occurred.

The plea was entered, and as expected, it was a plea of not guilty. This was usually the case. The mode of trial chosen was by judge alone. I figured I knew his reasons for not wanting a jury trial. When all the evidence was submitted, a jury of twelve of his peers, ordinary members of the general public, may be a little less understanding than a learned judge, who would have likely dealt with most every type of crime and heard all types of evidence during their tenure.

Then and there, the presiding judge and both lawyers conferred as to convenient dates for everyone concerned, and a week was set aside several months down the road. A week was felt to be adequate, but there would be no problem with an extension if it was necessary. He was remanded in custody. There would be no more bail hearings.

Meanwhile, the meetings with Crown counsel at the Confederation Building in St. John's continued. More interviews and re-interviews, more pictures, more memories and restless nights for everyone, especially the family of the deceased. I virtually relived everything over and over again. The facts and the upcoming trial were uppermost in my mind. I awoke too many times to count in a cold sweat, reliving what I had seen on March 13. I prayed that when the trial was over and justice was served, everything would settle down for me and I could put it to bed. I was wrong.

Again the time flew by. All the evidence for and against was in, and Monday was set for summations from both sides. I didn't attend. I had a couple of days off, and I just wanted to relax and put it all out of my mind. I knew no decision would be made at that time, as the judge would need time to consider all the evidence and would postpone to another date for his adjudication. I really didn't want to hear the summations, anyway. I had heard enough. For me, it was over. At least, that's what I thought.

CHAPTER 10
TRIAL AND VERDICT

This was it. The big day. In a few hours we would all know the verdict, guilty or innocent, and then the sentence. I never closed my eyes the whole night, going over everything, wondering if we had done enough. The judge asked very few questions of the witnesses during the trial, which I thought was good. What would be the final outcome? Had there been errors in giving evidence, which would benefit the accused? I regretted not attending the summations. The Crown-appointed lawyer for Mr. Butt had done a credible job representing his client. He was excellent in the way he questioned his own witnesses and in cross-examining the Crown's. However, I didn't think he had very much to work with. We also knew that Butt would never take the stand.

In contrast to the morbidly freezing night, morning, and day in March, today was hot and humid. The temperature was in the eighties, with the same forecast for the whole week.

Dressed in uniform—red serge, high browns, and breeks—I was extremely uncomfortable. However, that was the required dress for all uniformed members of the RCMP giving evidence in Supreme Court matters. Mr. Butt was brought for court from Her Majesty's Penitentiary in town in the rear of a marked police car, flanked by two other RCMP officers also in dress uniform. They were assigned guard duty. They had to ensure the prisoner was escorted to and from court safely and on time, and further to sit next to him during the trial, one on each side, in chairs situated just outside the box. The order of witnesses was the decision of the Crown prosecutor, who was well-versed in such matters. Being the first member on the scene, and due to the rest of my involvement, including, of course, the statement, I was to be the first witness. We were ready to go.

Right before court began, we had a brief meeting with the Crown prosecutor in a small office made available to him. It was then for the very first time I heard from his lips that the charge would be amended from first-degree murder to second-degree murder. I was shocked. Devastated. I couldn't believe it. I knew it was his choice, and his alone, but I couldn't believe what I was hearing. No one else appeared surprised. Maybe they had been aware of what was going to happen—they had been in St. John's and attended many more meetings than I had.

The difference, as I knew it, was that in order to prove murder in the first degree, the Crown had to prove beyond a shadow of a doubt that the murder had been planned and premeditated by the accused. The sentence, if convicted, would be life without the possibility of parole for at least twenty-five years. In second-degree murder it was not necessary to prove premeditation, just that a murder was committed and that the accused was the murderer. The sentence could be anything and was totally the judge's decision. Crown and defence lawyers did make recommendations before sentencing, but when all was said and done, it was up to His Honour.

A life sentence is not actually life. It's ten years, and parole can be granted at any time, usually after a third of the sentence has been served. That decision is made by a government-appointed parole board, usually three members, at predetermined meetings with the offender.

During the next week, member after member, witness after witness, specialist after specialist was called into the courtroom. It ended five days later. Every day the courtroom was filled to capacity. There were officers who were off-duty and wanted to sit in on the trial, the general public who were following the trial, the press, and witnesses who had given their evidence.

When I was called, I said a quick prayer on the way to the stand, which made me relax. I had given evidence hundreds of times before in all courts, Supreme Court included, so I was not the least bit nervous. As I took the stand and faced the full courtroom, I glanced at the accused. I had told myself that I wouldn't, but I did. He looked back at me, smiled, and nodded his head twice, like he was just saying hello and that everything was going to be all right.

I answered many questions from both sides, and I was confident that everything went well. I knew everything by heart and rarely had to refer to my written notes. We had a strong case, but still there were no guarantees. We were all satisfied that we had done our very best. I was convinced we would get the conviction that Mrs. Callan and her family deserved.

My thoughts wandered, and for some reason I was thinking back to a few years earlier, when I was first appointed Crown prosecutor for the RCMP. At that time, RCMP officers appointed by the detachment commander represented the Crown as any prosecuting lawyer would today, responsible for all summary matters under the Criminal Code, the Highway Traffic Act, and family matters. I was also one of a few RCMP officers at the time who had a special designation that enabled me to attend first appearances for several of the federal statutes, the Customs and Excise Act and the Wildlife Act. These special appointments were the first to be given to RCMP officers. I qualified due to the fact that in 1980 I had spent seventy-four days at sea with seven other RCMP officers aboard the CSS *Hudson*, enforcing the regulations as they pertained to the seal hunt during the time of the Greenpeace interruptions at the front. For this to be possible, we were all sworn in as federal fishery officers—there's a book in itself.

Due to the heavy workload on all government-appointed lawyers, we were a great help, as we were permitted to appear on the Crown's behalf for all first appearances. I really enjoyed my couple of years in this position. Mind you, this didn't distract from my other duties. I studied all court files to ensure there would be no problems the next day. I was ready. I remembered that first day as if it were yesterday. I laugh even now when I think about it, but rest assured that what happened was far from funny. It proves that when mistakes are made in court, some guilty persons go free. Each file was just as important as the next. It was now my responsibility to ensure that all the evidence on file was entered as it should be.

The sitting magistrate would hear the summary evidence on guilty pleas and render a verdict and penalty the same day. All not guilty pleas were set over at another time convenient to everyone. I was proud as could be, standing before the bench in my brown serge. Duty counsel was present and seated next to me. As it was my first time, I was a tad nervous but did an excellent job in hiding it. Even though I had given evidence in all courts many times, this was different.

"All rise. I declare this court opened in the name of Her Majesty the Queen. Please be seated."

My first file was a routine impaired driving charge, and the only witness for the Crown would be the arresting officer, who also happened to be the Breathalyzer technician. The defendant was called and entered a guilty plea. Nothing could have been easier, or at least that's what I thought. The officer took the stand and gave excellent evidence as to the circumstances resulting in the charge.

"Thank you," I said. "No further questions, Your Honour."

I sat down. The officer was supposed to leave the stand and sit back in the courtroom, or he could leave altogether, but he didn't move. He was just standing there looking at me. What was he waiting for? I had no idea, but I knew it was something I hadn't done. My mind was a total blank.

"No more questions, Your Honour," I repeated. "Thank you, Constable. You may step down."

There was dead silence. The judge looked at me in a way

that convinced me I had omitted something. I stalled and went back through the file. The magistrate knew, the duty counsel knew, the officer knew—but I didn't have a clue. The magistrate's voice broke the silence.

"Constable, is there anything else?"

I was in panic mode, soaked with sweat, drops of it falling on the table. I wished I could fall through the floor. In desperation, I asked if I could have a ten-minute recess. One word: no. My first case was gone.

"If there is no more evidence from the Crown, I change the plea to not guilty and dismiss the charge. The Crown failed to introduce the Breathalyzer certificate as evidence, which is an absolute must. You're free to go. Now, Constable, we'll take a ten-minute recess."

I moved the file to one side, and there it was, in plain view on the desk in front of me. I had picked it out before court to introduce it but totally forgot about it. How stunned could anybody be? Without the certificate, a true copy which had to be given to the accused—as proof that two samples were taken according to the law exhibiting the breath sample readings taken at the time—was null and void. No certificate, no evidence, no conviction. My mistake allowed a guilty man to walk out the door. And an impaired charge at that! The court reconvened, and we finished out the day without incident. As expected, back at the office, I ate a lot of crow. Several dismissal reports with reasons attached had to be filled out and filed with several departments, including RCMP headquarters. That was that. I managed to survive to fight another day. Ironically, the same officer picked up the same man two weeks later. This time he was convicted and was sentenced to two weeks in jail.

I was off-duty, but I wouldn't miss this for anything. Court was set for two o'clock. I left Whitbourne at twelve to give me lots of time to get there. I drove the forty-plus miles to Brigus in a marked police car. I just took my time. It was a beautiful late summer's day and very warm. I wasn't in a hurry. I was very thankful to be out of dress uniform and in proper civilian clothes, suit and tie. No doubt this was going to be a long afternoon.

On arrival at the courthouse, I couldn't help but notice that there were already a couple of dozen people standing around outside the locked front door, smoking and talking to each other. I thought they must all be from around the area, as they all appeared familiar with each other. They had probably followed the trial from the beginning—a big thing for the Brigus area.

A single door at the side on the rear of the building was for staff, lawyers, and police. I assumed that it doubled as a fire exit. Inside was a hall with two interior doors. One led to several offices, and the other opened into the courtroom. The security guard let me in after I showed him my police ID. I was thinking it was a good, secure system for back then. I stood in the empty courtroom, getting my bearings. I could hear the sounds of staff coming from their working area in the rear but saw no one. The guard remained at the door.

The courtroom in Brigus was quite large. At the back was an elaborate and beautifully designed judge's bench. It was located just a couple of feet from a door leading to his private office. The door was on the right as you looked out over the courtroom from the bench. There was no opening on the other side. The bench was several feet higher than the rest of the floor plan, and when seated he could clearly see everything that went on in his courtroom. In front of the bench was a ten-foot table used by the court clerks. To its left, again looking out, was the witness box. Eight feet or so in front of the clerk's desk was another smaller desk, eight feet in length, with three identical podiums separated equally for the use of the attending lawyers. Six feet behind that was the prisoner's dock, measuring three feet wide by four feet long, with one gate on its left facing the bench. Behind the dock, a rail with matching wood spindles about three feet high ran the full width of the courtroom, with a single swinging gate in the middle. Behind that was a large seating area. Finally, there was a line of ten individual chairs along the wall on the left side of the bench. These were not accessible to the general public.

I went back outside to have a cigarette. Just what I needed while I waited for everyone else to arrive from town. When I got outside, the crowd had more than doubled. It was quarter past one. *It won't be long now*, I thought as I lit my cigarette. I noticed an older gentleman walk toward me, and I kind of looked away. I really didn't want to talk to anybody.

"Hey buddy, how about one of your smokes?"

I didn't say a word, just took out the package and gave him one. I remember thinking that lately I was giving away more cigarettes than I smoked myself. At one thirty the front doors opened, and the crowd quickly filled the sixty or seventy available seats inside. They were quiet, only making some low chatter. I compared their entrance to what you would hear in church before the service started.

A marked RCMP blue and white Suburban pulled up to the side of the building, and six officers got out. I joined them. All six had in one way or another been involved in the investigation. We stayed outside for a few minutes and exchanged greetings. It wasn't necessary to talk about the verdict. We all knew where the others stood, and we were all of the same opinion—guilty. Neither one of us would hazard a guess on the penalty. When the charge was amended, I knew then and there that I wouldn't be content with whatever sentence was imposed.

The two uniformed officers with the prisoner were hanging a short ways back until the last minute, around 1:55 p.m. I thought it was a good idea. Better safe than sorry, as they say. The Crown and defence lawyers arrived with their staff a couple of minutes apart. All entered the courtroom via the side door, and the place was full. Several people were forced to remain outside, as there was just nowhere else to sit. If someone left, they never got back in, and their seat was filled by one of those waiting outside. The court security made sure that everyone was aware of the rules before court started.

When the rear doors closed, a uniformed RCMP member from St. John's Detachment was posted there to make doubly sure all the rules were followed. The ten seats along the wall were quickly filled by RCMP officers. Those who couldn't get a seat performed other guard-related duties to assist the court. There was not a word of objection from any court personnel.

I didn't pay much attention to who was actually sitting in the courtroom. My mind was elsewhere. I didn't notice anyone from the victim's family—not that I expected to. They had all been through hell and back as it was. Someone may have been there without me knowing. I only knew Phyllis because of my dealings with her. I looked at the floor, closed my eyes, closed out everything else, and concentrated only on the sounds around me. Something I did quite often—I found it very relaxing. A gentle nudge in the side by the officer sitting next to me brought me back to the moment. In a very low whisper, just barely loud enough for me to hear, he said, "Tom, your buddy's here."

I didn't comment. When I looked up, Guy Butt was seated in the prisoner's box, about ten feet in front of me, flanked by two RCMP officers in full dress uniform, one seated on either side. This time, they had worn their full Sam Browne belts, which holstered a loaded six-shot .38 Smith & Wesson, a handcuff pouch, and a second small leather pouch which contained two six-round speed loaders.

The prisoner was always handcuffed from behind, until he was put in the box. He must have felt me looking his way, because he immediately turned and looked into my eyes. He half-smiled and nodded. Life didn't seem to be treating him so badly: he was clean-shaven, he'd had a recent haircut, and he was wearing some nice civilian clothes. He also looked as if he had gained ten pounds.

Butt looked around the courtroom. His attention was drawn to some people in the first row on the right side of the room, right behind the rail. I had to look twice. It couldn't be! But it was. I hadn't seen her in a long time. I couldn't see Guy's face, as his back was to me. He was told to sit down, and he did, while looking her way. I couldn't believe it. The last time I had seen her was in Harbour Grace. I wouldn't have recognized her if I passed her on the street. She was totally different. In her own right she was a fine-looking young woman. She looked older, her face was drawn, and the only makeup she appeared to have on was red lipstick. She had lost a lot of weight and was wearing clothing that I had seen before but which were now too big for her. Her hair was long and straight and appeared to be brushed back in a ponytail.

I felt sorry for her. I always had, and that is most likely why I gave her husband so many liberties while at Whitbourne. She was a nice person, polite and respectful. Honestly, I was a little surprised to see her there. I thought for sure she would have left him, considering what he had done. I never knew if they had seen each other while he was in St. John's. A strange thought crossed my mind: which one of them was really the prisoner?

After everyone was seated, the place was quiet except for some poor soul in the back with some kind of a persistent cough. He was trying his best to muffle it but wasn't having much success. I was relieved I wasn't setting next to him. After laying his papers on the desk in front of him and pulling his chair forward, with both arms folded and resting on the desk, the judge acknowledged and thanked the Crown and defence lawyers for their professionalism. He thanked the witnesses for their honesty and forthrightness in giving evidence under difficult circumstances. Lastly, he thanked the gallery for the respect they showed the court throughout the trial by the order they maintained.

With his glasses perched precariously on the edge of his nose, looking over them and directly at the prisoner, the judge called him by his name. "Mr. Butt, would you please stand."

He complied, as did both lawyers. This was it, what we had

all been waiting for. It would soon be over for us, but never for the Callan family. As much as I wanted to, I just couldn't look up. My heart was pounding so much, I instinctively held my wrist and counted the beats in my pulse.

Looking directly at the prisoner, the judge explained to him the way things were about to unfold in order to ensure that he was fully aware of the procedure. The judge then asked him if he understood, and Guy indicated that he did.

"Thank you, Mr. Butt. Please be seated."

The judge then started his review of the evidence that had been presented during trial. He was succinct, accurate, and to the point. I was taking in every word. He continued with his summary, slow and methodical, easy to follow. Fifteen minutes into it, he paused for a drink of water and motioned to the bailiff to approach the bench. He whispered something and continued with his address to the court. By and by, I noticed that the coughing had stopped. I was totally engrossed in the judge's delivery.

A judge's concern is to ensure that what he has to say is heard clearly and fully and that it is understood by the prisoner and the lawyers attending. Judges have to follow the letter of the law. Every word he speaks is recorded verbatim, by hand and by machine. Later, it's transcribed into one complete document, word for word. The finished product, which in some cases can take months to process, will be made available to access when needed. All statements of fact and reasons and decisions given by judges in every trial has to stand the test of law. When it does, it becomes what is then referred to as case law. Case law simply means that what has previously been recorded at trial can be used at any time by a lawyer, judge, or magistrate as a reference at any other trial down the road. Case law rulings can be used for or against an accused person. However, if any statement made by the judge is appealed by the Crown or defence, that statement will not under any circumstances be referred to in any court as case law, until it has been affirmed by the Newfoundland Supreme Court of Appeals. It could even reach the Supreme Court of Canada for clarification. When and if the appeal passes every test of law, meaning that the law was followed to the letter, then and only then will it be considered as case law.

No one moved. Mrs. Butt and the two older people with her, whom I later found out were Guy's parents, never moved. I glanced her way several times. Each time her head was down and she was looking at the floor. For a fleeting second I thought about the poor fellow with the cough. It had stopped, and now I knew why. There was an empty seat in the back of the courtroom. I now knew what the judge had whispered to the bailiff.

The judge continued. It was 3:42 p.m. It was now over six months since March 13 had come in like a lion. After straightening some papers on his desk, and a quick sip of water, the judge removed his glasses, sat upright, and looked directly at the prisoner.

"Mr. Butt, could you please stand."

As before, lawyers and guards stood with him.

"Guy Butt, after carefully considering all the evidence presented against you in this matter before the court, I find you . . ."

The silence was deafening. Everything appeared to be moving in slow motion. Mrs. Butt continued looking at the floor. His parents looked troubled. They didn't look at each other in any way, just stared at the back of their son's head.

I felt bad for them, too. Guy was far from being a model son. He always seemed to be in some sort of trouble. It had started when he was living in Badger, forcing the family to move to Long Cove. I was aware of the things he did, some more cruel than others, but nothing that came close to this. All he ever had were drinking buddies, no real friends.

Rest assured that there were serious warning signs from the time he was eleven and living in Badger, clear indicators that there was something seriously out of order with his thinking process. Several years later, while living in Long Cove, naked, he poured paint over his entire body from head to toe. He didn't have any idea how life-threatening this could have been. Paint, as oil on birds, seals the pores of your skin. When your skin can't breathe, you can die. He began to drink at a very early age— never sociably but always to get drunk. The first to arrive and the last to leave.

"I find you, Guy Butt, guilty as charged. Do you wish to say anything before sentencing?"

EPILOGUE

It was over. For a long time it had been me against him, cop against criminal. All the other officers had done a fantastic job, just what was expected of them, but to me this was personal: Tom Gruchy against Guy Butt. Did I win? No. I was out to see that justice was served. Was justice served? What was important to me now was what the Callan family thought. Guy Butt had gotten fourteen years for a life taken.

The courtroom emptied as fast as it had filled up and not nearly as quiet. I didn't feel satisfied. I just had an empty feeling inside, like something was missing. When I left the room, I shook hands with the court guard. I was the first one in and the last one out. We never talked.

Mrs. Callan, I'm truly sorry. I feel the system let you down. Guy Butt's free, and now so are you, Minnie. God will be the final judge. He will not forget. Justice will be served. You can bet eternity on it.

A year after Guy Butt was sentenced for murder and sent to a federal prison, Mrs. Guy Butt became pregnant for him. Yes, believe it or not, he became a father while in prison. They say the housing units inside prison walls for conjugal visits have everything. Obviously they do—everything, that is, except birth control. The Butts were frequent users of the free accommodations. I wondered what they would say when asked by their child where he or she was conceived.

Fourteen years is hardly a death sentence. The system is what it is, and we have to live with it. Fourteen years, out in seven, and a baby on the way his first year in federal prison. A new life in a new province. I know where. Thank God it's not Newfoundland—our loss, and now their problem.

ACKNOWLEDGEMENTS

A very special thank you to my next-door neighbours, Mr. Kevin Saunders, whose father was a former police office, and Mr. Richard Power, a retired teacher and an astute, well-educated dear friend. As well, a thank you to Diana Gruchy, wife of my cousin Ted, who is an avid book reader. To all the others who read the first couple of chapters, thank you. Your opinions mattered.

To my wife, Mary, what can I say? Words on paper are only words that mean very little until they form a sentence. Mary has spent many hours reading my words over and over again and turned them into the sentences you're reading. She believed in me and kept me going when I wanted to quit so many times. Months trying to put this on paper turned into a couple of years.

To my wife's parents, Walter and Sadie Bishop, thank you for reading. Your approval was important to me.

Donna, Christina, Michael, Vanessa—you all lived with me through this way back then, and I thank you for putting up with me as long as you did. I love you all.

Last but not least, to my mother, Gertrude Gruchy (née Ennis)—thanks, Mom. I love you.

APPENDIX
SCENE PHOTOGRAPHS

All photographs were taken by me in the summer of 2013.

The harbour—650 feet deep in the centre. Two boys drowned here while on a small plastic raft. I was the lead investigator. One was found weeks later; the other was never found. That's another story, but not from me.

The winding main road through three communities. To the left is the way home for the killer and where the blood spots led to his arrest.

A closer look at the turn in the road where the victim walked on her way home. Her daughter's house from where she left is a stone's throw away from the top of the turn.

Another view of the walk home.

The slipway location. All these years later, it is gone. The rocks to the left were two or three feet from where Guy Butt had his small wooden boat frozen on, as you would expect in March.

The point of land, a couple hundred feet from the slipway, around which Guy Butt intended to row around to get the body off the rocks and slip it into the ocean. Fortunately, he was arrested before the sun rose and before he could get the chance.

To the left leads to the ocean and the slipway, now gone after all these years. To the right is a 200-foot driveway off the end of the road, where Guy Butt lived and was arrested.

A continuation of the road past Guy Butt's house.

The same road where Guy Butt lived, approximately a quarter-kilometre long. The same in 2013 as it was in 1986.

The spot where I parked the police car. Also the path where the witness walked, where the victim walked on her way home, and where the attack took place.

The other side of the point which Guy Butt would have had to row around, if he were able to get his boat free, to pull the body off the rocks and let it slip into the ocean.

Where Guy Butt had beaten Minnie Callan and attempted to rape her in the freezing snow, and the path on which she was dragged to the bank's edge.

From the guardrail to the edge: fifty to sixty feet.

The area where Guy Butt waited, where the witness walked, the route Minnie Callan took, and where she was brutally attacked.

Where I fell in 1986—and fell again in 2013, when I was taking photos of the crime scene with my wife, Mary.

The scene the way it looked in 2013. Top left is where Minnie Callan was thrown over the edge to the rocks below.

A close-up of where the killer stood and where he threw the victim, while still alive, over the bank to the rocks below.

A close-up of the jagged rocks Minnie Callan landed on, the ones closest to the water.

Where I saw Minnie Callan for the first time.

Tom Gruchy was born in St. John's, Newfoundland and Labrador, in 1948, and graduated from Brother Rice. From 1969 to 1974, he worked several jobs before joining the Royal Canadian Mounted Police. His first posting, in April 1975, was in St. John's.

Tom has served as a municipal enforcement officer with the Town of Conception Bay South and the City of Mount Pearl, and he spent thirteen years in vehicle sales and as business manager for several local automobile dealerships. He fully retired in 2011.

The Murder of Minnie Callan is Tom Gruchy's first book.

Visit Flanker Press at:

www.flankerpress.com

https://www.facebook.com/flankerpress

https://twitter.com/FlankerPress

http://www.youtube.com
/user/FlankerPress